C000229732

MONSTERS
OF WEST VIRGINIA

Mysterious Creatures in the Mountain State

Rosemary Ellen Guiley

STACKPOLE
BOOKS

Published by
STACKPOLE BOOKS
5067 Ritter Road
Mechanicsburg, PA 17055
www.stackpolebooks.com

Printed in the United States of America

FIRST EDITION

Cover art by Marc Radle
Cover design by Tessa J. Sweigert

Library of Congress Cataloging-in-Publication Data

Guiley, Rosemary.
  Monsters of West Virginia : mysterious creatures in the Mountain State / Rosemary Ellen Guiley. — 1st ed.
     p. cm.
  Includes bibliographical references (p.   ).
  ISBN 978-0-8117-1028-2 (pbk.)
  1. Cryptozoology—West Virginia. 2. Monsters—West Virginia. 3. Animals, Mythical—West Virginia. 4. Parapsychology—West Virginia. 5. Curiosities and wonders—West Virginia. 6. West Virginia—Social life and customs. I. Title.
  QL89.G85 2012
  001.944—dc23
                     2011042282

CONTENTS

INTRODUCTION

y introduction to the supernatural side of West Virginia began well over a decade ago through my research of ghosts, witches, Mothman, and Fortean phenomena. *Fortean phenomena*, or *Forteana*, are so named after Charles Fort (1874-1932), an American journalist who made a second career of cataloging thousands of paranormal or anomalous phenomena, such as rains of frogs, fish, stones, dead birds, flesh, and snakes; mystifying religious experiences; floating balls of light in the night sky; spontaneous human combustion; UFOs; ghosts and poltergeists; and mysterious creatures and monsters. Fort never attempted to explain these phenomena, but used these examples to point out the limitations of scientific knowledge and the danger of dogmatic acceptance of "natural" laws, which the phenomena seemed to contradict.

Today researchers look for explanations of the phenomena. First we must eliminate natural explanations and then consider paranormal ones. For many years, I have considered monsters and mysterious creatures, as well as UFOs, ghosts, and unknown entities, to originate in parallel dimensions and break through into our dimension in certain places and at certain times.

I have spent a great deal of time in the Mountain State on the trail of entities, creatures, and all sorts of phenomena. Every state and region has its own stellar cast of supernatural creatures, and West Virginia is no exception. The country roads, rolling

1

mountains, and mysterious vibe of the landscape have a constant allure. I have interviewed many people in the state about their various supernatural experiences, and I have had the pleasure of meeting many of the foremost researchers who also have been intrigued by the activity there. I was privileged to have known John A. Keel, an outstanding Fortean researcher and ufologist, famous for his work on Mothman in West Virginia. John's visionary explanations were ahead of their time and now make increasing sense from the perspective of physics.

Those who are already familiar with my work—forty-seven books and counting—know that I like to cover the whole spectrum of paranormal activity, for everything winds up being interrelated in some way. Even though the focus of this book concerns "monsters" and "mysterious creatures," we must from time to time spill into the related topics of UFOs, extraterrestrials, ghosts, spirits, and witches and sorcerers. The paranormal is never a neat little pie chart cut up into colored, separate slices. Rather, it is a sliding landscape where one thing often blurs into another. While the term "monsters" conjures up horrific shapes and frightening experiences—and there are plenty of those in West Virginia—some of the mysterious creatures are shape-shifters, fairies, banshees, and creepy spectral beings who are not the ghosts of the dead.

Those of us researching the field depend on eyewitnesses for reports and data. Hard evidence of monsters is rare, but anecdotal accounts are valuable for their consistencies and patterns. If you have an experience, in West Virginia or anywhere, please send me a report at reguiley@gmail.com. Meanwhile, enjoy your visit on the spooky paranormal byways of West Virginia!

Mystery in the Mountain State

As states go, West Virginia is one of the smallest, ranking forty-first in size in the United States, with about 24,230 square miles. It may be small, but it is packed with lore and accounts of apparitions, poltergeists, witches, shape-shifters, Bigfoot, mysterious birds and creatures, strange lights in the sky, demon dogs, weird cats, and a host of unique entities that have both amazed and terrified many a witness. There are a number of factors why.

West Virginia is almost entirely mountainous—hence the name the Mountain State—and is the only state fully within the Appalachian region, with the Allegheny Mountains also in the north. The Appalachians are some of the oldest mountains on earth, dating back more than three hundred million years. The mighty Ohio River forms the state's western boundary against Ohio. Other states along its borders are Kentucky, Pennsylvania, Maryland, and Virginia. The remote, densely wooded mountains and hills and lonely hollows, called "hollers," offer the ideal habitats and hiding places for all things strange. The state is full of small towns and hamlets, many of which still retain an aura of insulation and leeriness of outsiders. Even the cities are small—Charleston, the state capital and the largest, has about fifty-three thousand residents.

The supernatural folklore is a blend of beliefs brought by immigrants primarily from England, Germany, Ireland, Scotland, and Italy, mixed with diverse Native American lore, and accounts of the face-to-face encounters with unknown creatures that have been passed down through the generations and reported in the media.

Prior to the arrival of the European settlers, the lands along the Ohio River were favorite hunting grounds for Native Americans. The early Native Americans were the Eastern Woodlands. Diverse bloodlines have included the Shawnee, Mingo, Cherokee, Delaware, Seneca, Wyandot, Ottawa, Tuscarora, Susquehannock, Huron, Sioux, and Iroquois, as well as Lakota, Blackfoot, Apache, Navajo, Choctaw, Cree, and Aztec. Although the Native Americans hunted there, they made no permanent settlements in West Virginia. They considered the land cursed and full of bad spirits. Perhaps they sensed thin boundaries between dimensions, or had experiences with frightening creatures.

In terms of paranormal activity and reports, West Virginia is quite an active state, according to cryptid researcher Lon Strickler of Baltimore, Maryland, who runs the PhantomsandMonsters.com website and monitors worldwide stories of the strange. Most West Virginia reports made to the website concern sightings of

Mothman, the state's most famous creature, but also cover the gamut of the unexplained.

West Virginia's Paranormal Profile

Mysterious creatures are usually encountered in remote areas, and as mentioned, West Virginia is full of lonely pockets. There are exceptions, of course—Mothman is one of the most notable, for its appearances in the town of Point Pleasant. The entire state forms what I have christened the "Appalachian Doorway," a paranormal hot zone of ongoing activity.

In my investigations over the years, I have found what many other researchers have noticed as well—there are certain geophysical traits that characterize most paranormal hot zones. Mountainous areas are one trait, and large waterways are another. The Ohio River Valley has a long history of paranormal activity. What is it about water that attracts or enhances the paranormal? Is it the ionization in the air? The energy generated by the rush of water? Large rivers, and even large lakes, usually have a paranormal pedigree.

West Virginia is an important coal-mining state, and coal-rich areas are riddled with tunnels—another marker of paranormal activity. Old folklore holds that openings from inner earth, such as mines, tunnels, and wells, provide pathways to the surface for all kinds of spirits and entities.

While none of these factors prove paranormal activity, of course, they are nonetheless part of a profile built by paranormal investigation. I believe that geophysical profiles contribute to something else: the opening of interdimensional doorways known as portals.

According to quantum physics, our dimension is but one of eleven that exist in a multidimensional reality. We are not in a universe, but a multiverse. Most of the time, the boundaries between dimensions prevent us from having bleed-through experiences, which is quite a good thing, considering the potential for disorientation and chaos.

However, there seem to be certain places where the boundaries are thin or even permeable—places where entities and the gods, so to speak, can be accessed. Caves, holes, subterranean passages, mountains, the roots of sacred trees, and reflective surfaces such as lakes and ponds have long histories as entry points to invisible realms. The ancients understood these places, and built temples, shrines, standing stones, and monuments at them. Certain places were known to foster good energy and some were full of bad energy that would bring illness, bad luck, and misfortune. Certain other places were guarded by beings and spirits of the land—the Romans called any such guardian a "genius."

Throughout history, human beings have experienced visions, meetings with entities, and distortions of time and space at these unusual places, which were regarded as doorways to the under-world, or to the land of the gods. A person could create an opening between worlds at these places by conducting the right rituals, making the right offerings, and being in the right state of con-sciousness.

People have also fallen through time and space accidentally. When they encounter a mysterious creature, an alien, or a spirit, they may be having an interdimensional experience. The creature may not exist in our world, but in another dimension. Under certain conditions, a portal opens and a sighting or an encounter occurs.

Other dimensions may explain the odd and sudden appear-ances of mystery beings and their ability to vanish in the blink of an eye. Most mysterious creature and paranormal experiences are brief, and some are so fleeting that the experiencer is left to won-der if it was only imagination.

Paranormal researchers have considered the other-dimensional explanations for several decades. Ufologist Jacques Vallee and folklorist Thomas E. Bullard were among the first to compare "extraterrestrials" to fairies and other unknown entities. Space beings may not be from outer space, but from inner space, part of our own multiverse.

John A. Keel, one of the greatest pioneers in research of UFOs and mysterious creatures, coined the term "ultraterrestrial" to describe these beings. Keel made history as the leading investigator of the Mothman sightings during the original wave in 1966 and 1967 in the Point Pleasant area.

Interdimensional portals make a great deal of sense in explaining the paranormal. If we are in the right place at the right time, and in the right state of consciousness, a portal can break open. West Virginia seems to be full of portal pockets, places where the boundaries between realms are thin or even open most of the time.

Speaking of being in the right place, here is a curiosity about encounters with mystery creatures. They are often seen late at night while someone is driving along a country road—and they go around a bend. Suddenly, there in the middle of the road, is a beast that is clearly not of this world. Sometimes the creatures are on the side of the road, but frequently they are smack in the middle, and often around a bend, not on a straightaway. Is there some peculiarity of portals and bends in interdimensional space that translates to bends in a road? Also, the creatures are often standing in the road, not moving or walking, as though they were dropped down a tube. When the vehicle comes into sight, they begin moving away, sometimes with astonishing speed.

There are many exceptions, of course, but I have noticed this characteristic reported frequently in eyewitness accounts.

Evaluating the Evidence for Creatures

One of the most vexing aspects of research into mysterious beings and phenomena is the difficulty in obtaining hard evidence. Beings that do not seem to belong in this reality elude capture in photographs and videos, and even capture of themselves. They seldom leave behind trace evidence, and what little is found is often tantalizing, but seldom convinces the scientific establishment.

Cryptozoologists tend to look for natural explanations, often believing that extraordinary creatures do exist, but are remnants of earlier species thought to be extinct. Survivors of the ancient past cannot be ruled out, but how do they remain so well hidden? Remote parts of mountains and forests have been cited as the habitats and resting places of monsters, but how long can such places remain remote and unexplored?

What about their feeding habits? Some creatures, such as Bigfoot, are seen foraging for food. Others, such as monster birds, seem to hunt for live prey, and dogmen have been seen eating roadkill. Why do we not see such hunters more often, not only from the ground but from the air?

Why do we find no carcasses or bones? Excrement and hair tufts associated with mysterious creature sightings have been found and analyzed—sometimes with the conclusion of "unknown"—and casts have been made of mysterious foot, paw, and claw prints.

The physical evidence for mysterious creatures is slim to none. We are left primarily with eyewitness accounts. While many are indeed compelling and difficult to refute, they are rarely backed up with hard evidence. The small amount of photographic evidence captured is continually debated, debunked, and dismissed, especially by the scientific community.

The lack of evidence makes sense if we consider these creatures to originate in another dimension. They are in our world for a fleeting time, and vanish into another space beyond our world.

Hoaxes and Hoax Journalism

In addition to slim evidence, researchers must contend with hoaxes and hoax journalism. Human beings have a bent for hoaxes, and there have been some good ones throughout history. One of the most famous and clever hoaxes was the Piltdown Man, fragments of a skull and bones said to be an early "missing link" human, found in Piltdown, England, in 1912. Forty years elapsed before the hoax was exposed.

There are clumsy hoaxes, too, such as the alleged frozen Bigfoot carcass found in Georgia in 2008, a case discussed in a later chapter. The hoax was exposed within days as the "Bigfoot" defrosted.

Newspapers themselves are not above hoaxing. The news media traditionally is supposed to search for and report the truth, but that is not always the case, especially when it comes to sensational stories. Tabloids today are renowned for fabulous and fabricated tales, but in the past reputable newspapers indulged in phony stories as part of their competition for readers and advertisers.

Hoax journalism arose in the early nineteenth century, with the advent of the "penny press," or cheaply produced newspapers. In order to garner sales, such publications ran serial novels and stories trumpeting wild headlines. In England, they were called "penny dreadfuls," a reflection on their quality. *Varney the Vampire*, a serial novel about an aristocrat-turned-bloodsucker, was a famous example. Such stories permeated the American press as well.

Some newspapers did not stop at fictional stories, however, but published fictional *news* stories. Many of them were of a supernatural nature: monsters seen, found, and killed; exotic life on the moon; and so on. Others dealt with Jules Vernesque technology. The gullible public gobbled them up, many believing such accounts to be real.

Even more astonishing than phony news itself were the writers of some of the tales—well-respected and even famous fictional authors. Some were having a lark, others needed the money. In 1844, Edgar Allan Poe, whose finances were always precarious, wrote a "news" story for *The New York Sun* about a balloon journey across the Atlantic. "The Balloon Hoax," as it came to be known later, had people paying scalper prices for copies of the *Sun*, which must have been an irony to the poverty-stricken Poe. Even Poe himself could not score a copy on the street.

Similarly, Mark Twain wrote a "news" story about a bizarre murder, and his friend William Wright, using the pseudonym Dan de Quille, concocted a tale of supernatural stones that, when separated, moved toward each other on their own.

Tales of sea serpents, werewolf beasts, flying dragons, giant birds, and so on that were reported in the nineteenth-century newspaper press have to be considered as possible hoaxes. Such accounts unfortunately muddy the waters of research, for people have had genuine sightings and encounters of unexplained creatures and phenomena. A handful of fabricated news articles do not negate all experiences and accounts, but they are land mines in a field that often struggles for credibility with science and the mainstream. Just ask any eyewitness brave enough to come forward and bear the ridicule of the press and "establishment," a plight well illustrated in some of the most famous monster cases in West Virginia.

Despite the hazard of hoaxes, there are plenty of real-deal cases everywhere, including West Virginia. A mysterious world lies close to the surface of the ordinary world there.

The Grafton Monster

ysterious creatures sometimes make a single dramatic appearance, creating a panic and then vanishing, never to be seen again—at least in that location. Witnesses are left to wonder where the creature came from, where it went, and why it ever showed up in the first place. So it was in 1964 with the Grafton Monster, a creature straight out of a horror or science-fiction film that made a sleepy little town famous.

Grafton is the seat of Taylor County in the north-central hills of the state. It embraces the Tygart River, and is about twenty-five miles south of Morgantown, twenty-one miles east of Clarksburg, and one hundred-fifty miles northeast of Point Pleasant, another town famous for a monster, Mothman. In its heyday Grafton was a wealthy mining center, and one of its biggest claims to fame is the founding of Mother's Day there in 1908. In 1964, it was a well-behaved town, the kind of place where big news was an occasional burglary or the shenanigans of teenagers. It was not the setting one might expect for the shocking appearance of a monster that fit no description of anything known on this planet.

On June 16, 1964, Robert Cockrell, a young reporter in his mid-twenties for the *Grafton Sentinel* (now called the *Mountain Statesman*) ended his evening shift around 11 P.M. He headed home in his car, driving along Riverside Drive, which follows the Tygart. Cockrell knew the road well and zipped along at about fifty miles an hour. He was for the most part alone on the road, for most residents were in bed by this hour. The night was clear, and Cockrell was in good spirits.

As he rounded a curve and entered a straight section of road about a mile long, his headlights caught something that he knew immediately was out of place. It appeared to be a "huge white obstruction on the right side of the road standing between the road and the riverbank on a cleared-off section of grass," as he related later.

Almost as soon as he saw it, he realized it was not an object but a "Thing," a beast the likes of which he had never before seen. It stood seven to nine feet tall and was about four feet wide. It was stark white, with slick, seal-like skin, or a covering that resembled sealskin. It had no head. As he passed it, the Thing did not move, but Cockrell could tell that it whatever it was, it was alive.

Terrified, and with cold chills racing up and down his spine, Cockrell slammed his foot down on the gas pedal and sped off. When he got home, he was tempted to barricade himself behind locked doors. After he calmed down, he realized that his duty as a reporter called for him to return to the scene to investigate. He recruited two friends, Jerry Morse and Jim Mouser, to accompany him.

When they arrived at the spot, however, the Thing was gone. They searched up and down the riverbank for more than an hour but found nothing. There were no tracks, although the grass where Cockrell had seen the creature had been mashed down by something quite heavy. It was as though the monster was there and then instantly not there, without ever leaving the area. While they searched, they heard an odd, low whistling sound coming from the direction of the river. The whistling seemed to follow them, but they could not see whatever was making the noise.

When Cockrell went to work the next day, he was reluctant to mention the sighting out of fear that he would be ridiculed as crazy, or that he would be accused of creating a hoax. Once again his sense of duty as a journalist prevailed, and he informed his editor. A small story written from a cynical point of view was published on June 18.

Word of the sighting raced through Grafton and soon created a monster-hunting sensation. More than one hundred teens and adults, armed with flashlights, mallets, crowbars, bats, and other crude weapons, thronged to the river at night in hopes of tangling with the "Headless Horror." More than twenty searchers said they saw it, including at the nearby stone quarry. Questioned individually by Cockrell, their accounts tallied "to the finest detail," he said. One youth oddly opined that the creature must be an "escaped polar bear," though he offered no explanation as to how a polar bear might arrive in Grafton on its own.

State, county, and local police were less impressed. Officers made a cursory search of the area and said they found nothing.

Though the newspaper played the incident down, gossip played it up, and the following night even more people turned out to monster hunt, clogging Riverside Drive with bumper-to-bumper traffic and scores of vehicles pulled off to the side. No one reported a sighting as dramatic as the one had by Cockrell, however.

In a second article published on June 19, the *Grafton Sentinel* dismissed the creature as a "wildly imaginative story" inspired by "a combination of spring fever, a lack of recreational facilities, and recent publicity given a Michigan town which claimed to have a 'monster' which followed people." The "Michigan Monster," however, was a Bigfoot-like creature that bore no resemblance to what Cockrell saw. The *Sentinel* article also suggested that the creature was actually a person pushing boxes around on a hand cart, who took on a "weird shape" in the darkness. Apparently there was a local woman known to push boxes around on a hand cart, but why she would have been out doing so at 11 P.M. along the river was not explained. Sometimes people who do not want to face the reality of the unknown come up with even more bizarre "natural" explanations.

The monster hunting died down, but Cockrell quietly pursued his own investigation. He found reports of the creature matching his description up and down the Tygart River, and as far north as Morgantown in advance of his sighting. He never published his findings. He contacted Gray Barker, a Clarksburg researcher of

UFO and paranormal phenomena, and exchanged correspondence with him about the case, firmly stating that the sighting was not a figment of his imagination, or a practical joke. Barker drove to Grafton to interview Cockrell, and intended to write the case up for a UFO magazine. Though he wrote a draft of an article, he never published it. He saved the letters, notes, and newspaper clippings, which are on file in the Gray Barker collection of papers housed in the Clarksburg Public Library.

Cockrell asked Barker for his explanation of the creature and received a letter with a novel answer:

> The most interesting facet of your report, to me, was the whistling sound heard from the direction of the river. I have a theory, which although it isn't generally accepted, is still interesting to me. When rocket ships from the U.S. reach an inhabited planet, or one which has some sort of reasonably breathable atmosphere, we will at first deposit experimental animals (probably monkeys) on the surface of the planet before getting out ourselves. These specimens will then be carefully retrieved and thoroughly examined to note effects of the alien environment on them. If space people are visiting us now, they might be doing the very same thing. Thus the whistling sound, if one fits it in with this theory, could well be the sound of the "flying saucer" retrieving its specimen—in this case the weird-looking monster.

In his draft article, Barker elaborated on his argument for test creatures:

> We will want to know the effects of an alien atmosphere will have upon them, whether there are any harmful radiations our instruments have not picked up; what the reactions of the alien residents will be if they have by chance sight [sic] the animal—and probably, more important, the effect of the local planetary viruses and bacteria to which earth fauna has not had an opportunity to adapt.

We would by [t]hat time have a very efficient system of retrieving the experimental animals, and if we wanted our observance to be made in secret, would excertise [*sic*] all caution to make sure the animal was not captured.

Are saucerians dropping experimental animals or "monsters" among us[?] To this reporter this is just as likely as is the present suspected visitations by otherplanetarians.

Barker may not have been off base with his idea of stalking-horse creatures to test out an alien planet environment. He does have a point—would not we do the same thing? His explanation of the whistling sound as the whirring of a spacecraft is more of a stretch, evoking the crude spinning saucers in the old science-fiction movies of his time. Most unknown craft sightings reported by people today are silent.

The Grafton Monster fits the model of an interdimensional traveler. Perhaps it entered our dimension and spent some time roaming about West Virginia. Odd sounds are often reported in entity encounters and may be a side effect of a transdimensional shifting. We should consider the possibility that the creature was intelligent and wished to avoid interaction with humans and so made itself invisible while Cockrell and his friends hunted the area. By the time the monster hunters descended in the next few nights, the creature was gone, either back into its own dimension or off somewhere else.

Cockrell found reports of sightings similar to his around the same time, but a curious story from 1952 indicates that the creature was no stranger to West Virginia and may have been around for quite some time. A sighting of it in late September that year was assumed to be related to the Flatwoods Monster case, which had occurred in Braxton County a couple of weeks earlier. A description of the white "washtub" entity bears no resemblance to anything seen in the Flatwoods case—but it does sound remarkably like the refrigerator-sized being seen in Grafton.

Thomas I. Stafford, who wrote a column called "Bug Dust" for the *Register* in Beckley, reported on September 21 the following sighting from a woman in Skelton. This creature moved energetically around and even hovered in the sky. Stafford treated the sighting in the flip fashion typical of the media:

> 'Tis said that the Flatwoods monster has moved on to Raleigh County—to the vicinity of the Greenbrier Dairy at that.
>
> Mrs. Earl Hutchinson, of Skelton, called to inform Bug Dust that she had seen a "shiny something" hovering in the sky some distance from her home. At first she thought it was a man in a parachute, but when it kept swinging back and forth and jumping up and down, she figured the Flatwoods monster was en route to Beckley—for a rendezvous with other monsters, no doubt.
>
> 'Twas a big white thing, resembling a washtub, but not being Monday Mrs. Hutchinson knew Ole Sol wasn't hanging out his dirty linen.

There are no further details of the creature's appearance, but it was shiny, white, shaped like a washtub, and did not seem to have a noticeable head, even though at first Hutchinson assumed it to be a man.

Skelton, in Raleigh County, lies about 150 miles south of Grafton. The Grafton Monster seemed to have quite a geographical range throughout the length of the state.

We will never know where the Grafton Monster came from, or where it went. There are plenty more creatures to keep us guessing, however, for West Virginia brims with the supernatural.

Monster Birds, Thunderbirds, and Flying Reptiles

In the fall of 2007, a man driving along a quiet county road in West Virginia had an encounter with a giant winged creature from either another realm or earth's distant dinosaur past. The entire encounter lasted only about ten to fifteen seconds, but it was long enough for details to be seared into his memory.

The unnamed man, who was interviewed by researcher Stan Gordon of Pennsylvania, was driving on a rural, two-lane road near Clenedin in Kanawha County around 8 A.M. Suddenly he had to slam on the brakes, for there in the middle of the road appeared a bizarre, enormous creature with wings, unlike anything he had ever before seen. It appeared to be feeding on roadkill, perhaps an opossum, and was tearing at it with a big black beak.

The man stared in amazement at the "bird," which stood at least four feet tall, its huge head higher than the roofline of his car. The beast seemed as shocked as the man was, and it pulled back its head on its long, crooked neck to stare at him with dark eyes. For a few moments, human and creature locked gazes.

The creature's body was covered with dark brown or black feathers, but the head was bald. Its neck was ringed with a collar of yellow-orange feathers. The legs were feather-covered, but the feet were bare. The upper torso was well muscled with shoulders.

After staring at the man for a few seconds, the creature turned and spread out its massive wings, which spanned the entire width of the road, and started a lumbering roll for takeoff. It ran away from the car in a jumping, hopping motion from foot to foot while flapping its wings, the tips of which stirred up dust and gravel from the road. Despite its awkward running, the bird did not seem panicked, and its wings flapped in a smooth, fluid motion. After about five yards, it lifted silently into the air. As it gained altitude, the wings appeared to be more like massive feathered arms, attached to the body the way human arms are connected to the torso. The creature vanished once it cleared the treetops.

Like many witnesses suddenly startled by the sight of a creature that "should not be," the man did not think to grab his cell phone and snap a photo of it. He resolved to travel with a video camera in case he saw it again—but like many similar encounters, they happen once and never again, at least not to the same person.

Later the man returned to the spot and measured the road. It was twenty-one feet wide. No known species of bird in the present has such an enormous wingspan. After doing some research, the closest creature he could find was a teratorn, a giant bird that lived millions of years ago and is supposed to be extinct. Others might have labeled the mystery creature a thunderbird, a giant of legend that seems to be more than imaginary. Where did this Clenedin creature come from? And how could such a large thing actually get off the ground and fly?

Giant birds dive bombing from the skies to snatch up animals, pets, and children for their next meal sounds like science-fiction horror. To unfortunate victims and witnesses all over the world, including West Virginia, such a scenario is not fantasy but reality. Bloodthirsty thunderbirds and prehistoric-looking flying monsters appear in modern skies, according to eyewitnesses. Are they long-lost species who manage to remain hidden most of the time—or do they swoop in from holes between dimensions or in the fabric of time itself?

The most famous of the giant mystery birds is the thunderbird, prominent in Native American lore and still flying today, according to eyewitness accounts. Thunderbirds are sighted all over North America. Pennsylvania seems to be "Thunderbird Central" in the numbers of modern sightings, which extend into surrounding states, including West Virginia. To appreciate the fascinating and complex phenomenon of giant mystery birds, we will venture a bit beyond the state borders in our exploration of them. Giant bird and birdlike creatures also are related to West Virginia's most famous mysterious creature, Mothman.

We know from fossils that giant birds are real, and once ruled the skies during the age of dinosaurs. Not all flying things were birds—the earliest vertebrate beasts to take to the air were reptiles. The meat-eating pterosaurs, or "winged lizards," soared around on leathery wings of stretched membrane up to forty feet in span. Their long jaws were full of teeth, and they had long tails. Some had fur-like filaments covering their bodies. Their bones were hollow, which aided their ability to fly. They must have been a fearsome sight in the sky, especially when hunting.

Pterosaurs lived from 220 million to 65.5 million years ago, during the late Triassic and Cretaceous periods. They are sometimes generally called pterodactyls, which are but one type of pterosaur. Even though pterosaurs are officially extinct, modern people have sightings of flying creatures that bear striking resemblances to them. Some of those sightings have occurred in West Virginia.

Pterosaurs eventually gave way to feathered creatures. The largest known flying bird from prehistoric times is the *Argentavis magnificens*, named from fossils discovered in Argentina. This flying wonder was eleven feet long and weighed between 160 and 170 pounds. Wings spanning twenty-five feet were necessary to get this bird off the ground. Ornithologists, experts on birds, today think that it would be hard, even inconceivable, for such a massive creature to get off the ground. Nonetheless, the creature had the right bones and build for taking off.

Other giant birds were the previously mentioned teratorns, predators with wingspans up to twenty-five feet and long, hooked beaks that enabled them to grab hold of small animals, which they most likely swallowed whole. Teratorns ("monster birds") were birds of prey that lived in North America and South America in the Miocene period, five million to eight million years ago. Today's condors are related to them. They were dark-feathered birds with narrow, hooked beaks and collars of white feathers around the neck.

By contrast, even the giants of today are much smaller. The bird with the largest wingspan is the wandering albatross, at up to eleven feet. The heaviest bird of prey is the condor, weighing an average of twenty to twenty-five pounds, with a wingspan of about ten feet. And the heaviest bird that can fly is the bustard, weighing in at about forty pounds. No wonder scientists say that monster flying birds simply cannot exist.

Legends and myths the world over tell of giant birds who seem fantastical, but may actually be based on real experience. Perhaps our distant ancestors witnessed remnants of huge species long gone and told stories about them that became more embellished over time. Giant birds are universal in mythology, legend, and lore. Some of them are predatory, feeding on large animals and humans.

The roc of ancient Arabian and Persian lore was so big that it could carry people on its back, according to the stories in *The Book of 1001 Nights*, also known as *Arabian Nights*. Sinbad the Sailor rode one, and he was so dwarfed by the size of the bird that the creature did not even know he was there on its back. In 1298 the explorer Marco Polo said the roc looked like an enormous eagle and was strong enough to carry off an elephant.

Related to the roc was the Persian *simurgh*, or "dog bird," having the body of a lion, the head of a dog, and the wings and talons of an eagle. Eagle-like giants were the *garuda* of India and Indonesia and the *imgig* of Sumer.

Thunderbirds are the legendary giant birds prominent in North American lore, appearing in Native American mythologies across the land. In the Pacific Northwest, thunderbirds sit atop the totem poles of local tribes.

Thunderbirds are so named because they are storm bringers. Thunder sounds from the flapping of their wings and lightning issues from their eyes. Thunderbirds carry off people, animals, and even whales, according to legends. They bear a resemblance to eagles and vultures, and have long necks, long hooked beaks from which protrude teeth, and white tufts around their necks and sometimes their wingtips. Their hidden homes are in the mountains and remote areas. Are they legendary or real? They may be a bit of both—legend based on centuries of real experiences and sightings.

One of the most dramatic thunderbird encounters in modern times, worthy of note even though it happened in another state, occurred in 1977 in Lawndale, Illinois. On July 28, a giant bird thought to be a thunderbird lifted a ten-year-old boy off the ground in front of witnesses, including his mother. Marlon Lowe was playing in his backyard with two friends on that evening. Around 8:30 P.M., two huge birds sailed over the yard. One of them swooped down and seized Marlon, lifting him about two feet into the air. Marlon screamed and punched at the bird. After flying about thirty-five feet, the bird dropped him to the ground. His mother, Ruth, responded to his screams, and saw him aloft in the air. After dropping Marlon, the two birds flew off and were not seen again.

Ruth Lowe notified the police and a game warden, concerned that other children might be at risk. In return, the Lowe family was ridiculed in the media and by "experts" who stated flatly that there was no bird in existence that could lift a sixty-five-pound child into the air. The story simply was not true. As for Ruth Lowe, she stated later that if she had the chance to do it all over again, she would not tell anyone.

There was a wave of sightings of huge birds around the time of the Lawndale incident, a wave that was by no means the first in the Midwest—or elsewhere in North America. No matter what the "experts" want to believe, big birds that can grab a child are not the stuff of imagination.

The "Roc" in West Virginia

West Virginia has been home to giant birds, the sightings of which continue to this day. Many of them have been in conjunction with Mothman, the state's celebrity creature.

In 1895, residents of Addison, now known as Webster Springs, were terrorized for weeks by a giant predatory bird dubbed by the press as "a modern Roc," according to a newspaper account. The bird, which screamed like a panther, reportedly carried off a dog and a fawn, wounded a hunter, and was blamed for the disappearance of a ten-year-old girl.

A long report of the avian attacks was published on February 24, 1895, in the *St. Louis Globe-Democrat*. The bird was described both as a man-sized giant and as an eagle. According to the account, the following episodes occurred.

The ten-year-old daughter of a man named Dan Junkins, a resident of Bergoo, suddenly disappeared, and locals blamed the giant bird as the culprit. Landry Junkins was sent out by her mother one Friday afternoon to go to a neighbor's cabin one-and-a-half miles away to ask about the wife, who was ill. She set out on foot around noon and was never seen again. A search party found her tracks, which ended about a half-mile from the neighbor's cabin. From the crazy directions of the prints, it appeared that she might have been trying to avoid something.

A bear hunter named Peter Swadley was badly wounded and his dog was carried off by the big bird. Swadley and his hunting dog, Gunner, were in the Piney Ridge area, which Swadley knew well. They entered a clearing and, without warning, were attacked by a screaming giant bird the size of a man. The bird buried its talons into Swadley's back, tearing his coat to shreds. The two tussled in the snow, and twice Swadley, a powerful fighter in his own right, was lifted off his feet. The bird gashed his forehead over his left eye. Swadley was certain the bird would have torn him to bits had it not been for the intervention of Gunner. The bird ripped open the dog's stomach, grabbed it in its claws, and flew away. Swadley was nearly blinded by the streaming blood from his eye wound, but he was able to make his way down the mountain to Laurel Creek, where he found the cabin of Abe Kitsmiller. Kitsmiller treated his wounds and took him into Addison for additional medical treatment. The article described him as in "precarious condition."

On another day, a Webster County deputy sheriff and his son witnessed the bird carry off a fawn. Rube Nihiser and son Hanse, who lived near Spruce Creek at the foot of Owl Head Mountain, went off on a deer hunt. They found the tracks of a doe and fawn and followed them across Piney Ridge to Sugar Run. As they reached a clearing, they heard "ear-splitting screams." They hurried on and then saw the doe and fawn being stalked by a giant bird wheeling over them in the sky. The bird dive-bombed the doe and then the fawn repeatedly. The doe tried valiantly to defend her fawn, but the bird grabbed it and flew off. Nihiser fired his rifle at it, but if a bullet struck it had no effect. The bird took off in the direction of Snaggle Tooth Knob, where many locals believed the bird to have its nest. Nihiser described the bird as "of immense size, and that its spread of wings must have been fully fifteen or eighteen feet. Its body . . . was as large as that of a man, and its cries were loud and shrill in the extreme. The feathers were of a dark brown color, with white on the wings, and light underneath. Its eyes were tremendous, larger than those of the largest-sized owl, and they shone with tremendous brilliancy, plainly discernible."

Hanse Harder, who maintained a sheep ranch on Rattlesnake Run, was convinced that the "eagle" flew off with one of his sheep and spooked the rest of the flock. Harder was housing the sheep in a shed because of the harsh winter. One day he and his wife left for the day, and when they returned Harder discovered one of his sheep was missing, and the rest were frightened. There was a large hole in the shed's roof with bits of wool clinging to the edges. There were no tracks around the shed to indicate either an animal or human thief. Convinced that the predator was a "harnt," or spirit, Harder fixed the roof and made a small cross out of hemlock boughs, which he nailed around the shed and over his cabin door. Hemlock is believed to have the power to repel evil spirits. There were no more attacks.

Other residents claimed to have seen a giant bird in the vicinity of Snaggle Tooth Knob, a formidable mass of sheer crags and cliffs resembling a crooked front human tooth, and covered in winter by ice. Some of the accounts were dismissed even by locals as "moonshine stories," but one of the oldest mountaineers, "Pap" Tammen, stated that "many years ago" the area had been invaded by two giant birds who came in winter, lived at Snaggle Tooth Knob, stole livestock, and then disappeared in the spring.

The article concluded with the unknown fate of Landy Junkins, who was assumed to have been carted off to Snaggle Tooth Knob.

It is difficult to assess the account, written in the purple prose characteristic of the times. Was this article another one of those nineteenth-century journalistic hoaxes? It is odd that the story was published in St. Louis, not in Addison, or even in West Virginia. If there were any follow-up reports, such as one might expect concerning the missing girl, none surfaced.

The story may have been hoax journalism to attract readers. Even if fictional, however, the story nonetheless contains elements present in modern-day experiences, notably the Lawndale, Illinois, attack.

Whether or not the Webster County dramas took place as reported, the area around Snaggle Tooth Knob and parts of Webster County have had multiple sightings of unusually large birds over a period of years. The birds appeared in wintertime, when food is scarce.

Were they large eagles or other ordinary birds of prey, or were they thunderbirds or mystery birds? Hoax press or no, West Virginia has been home to many unusual bird sightings.

A "Prehistoric" Bird

In 1970, two people from Maysville in Grant County witnessed a massive bird that, like the Clenedin bird, had a wingspan as wide as the road. The daylight sighting took place in the mountains, in an area associated with sightings of Bigfoot and humanoid cryptids.

The witness, whose gender is not given in the report, said that he or she was driving with his or her mother up a mountain road, and they were followed by the mystery bird:

We saw only the tail and the underside of this animal. Its wings were almost as wide as the road. This animal repeatedly flew over the hood of the car as we drove. It did not have a feathered tail—its tail looked long and coiled up. It was dark in color.

When we witnessed this I told my mother that it looked like a prehistoric bird. This animal was much larger than a turkey, turkey buzzard, owl, eagle, hawk or any other bird of prey that I have ever seen. It had a broad heavy body. In fact it looked so large that it had trouble getting airborne and it used the path of the road to get up in the air. This bird looked large enough to easily take down a dog or deer-sized animal.

I cannot say that it had any man-like features but this was something that both myself and my mother still remember. I have to believe that other people witnessed what we saw and I can see why they called it Mothman. This is a true story—for obvious reasons I can see that people blow it off as untrue but we know the truth. I know another person in Maysville, WV that has described something similar. He explained to me he did not know what it was but it was as big as the highway is wide.

The absence of humanoid features rules out this creature as a cousin of Mothman; however, in the wake of the famous Mothman wave of 1966 and 1967, almost any flying oddity since then has been called "Mothman."

A Turkey-Legged, Pterodactyl-Headed, Winged Thing

This strange creature was spotted one night in February 1994 in Braxton County, where the famous Flatwoods Monster case took place in 1952. Was it a weird bird-animal combination or a mystery humanoid? Only one sighting was reported:

> Three men were out driving on an isolated country road. They rounded a curve and came upon a tall winged figure standing in the middle of the road. It had long, spindly, turkey-like legs, and it stared at the men with glowing eyes. After a few moments, it turned, rose up an embankment and vanished into the night. Later, one of the witnesses said he thought the creature's head looked like that of a pterodactyl.

Bighoot and Birdman

Giant owls or owl-like birds have frequently been reported in West Virginia and also farther to the west in the Ozark Mountains. Mark A. Hall, a cryptozoology researcher and author, has dubbed the creature or creatures "Bighoot," and has speculated that it might be a giant eagle-owl related to the genus *Bubo* and the great horned owl.

Giant owls existed in earlier times, even a mere few thousand years ago, according to fossils that have been found. Bones of an owl measuring a little more than three feet in height have been found in Cuba; the creature became extinct about 8,000 to 10,000 years ago. Native Americans all across the continent have folklore about supernaturally large owls, some with the bodies of humans.

Bighoots have been reported throughout southwestern West Virginia and in Ohio. The birds are described as several feet tall with wingspans up to ten feet. They have brown and gray feathers, are nocturnal, and have red eyeshine, which is characteristic of some owls.

Bighoot sightings have been mixed with sightings of other entities, one an owl-human creature called Birdman, and Mothman.

In 2002, when Mothman publicity heated up again with the release of the film *The Mothman Prophecies*, an Ashton woman told the *Huntington Herald-Dispatch* that her husband had shot and killed a giant owl during the Mothman flap. Betty Sturgeon said both she and her husband saw the giant bird, and at about the same time, their dog went missing. Husband Calvin thought the owl had killed it, and he would go out at night with his gun looking for the bird. Sturgeon said he shot it and buried it near their mobile home on Eighteen Mile Creek Road. In 1979, a new house was built on the spot. Calvin died in 1996.

Monster Birds

Ornithologists and other scientists often dismiss reports of giant birds, especially those that lift animals and children, as nonsense. They claim witnesses are lying, or are at best "mistaken," confusing known birds such as eagles, condors, owls, and herons for something more exotic. Many sightings probably go unreported, because either the witnesses are uncertain, they fear ridicule, or they are informed by others that the creatures are ordinary.

For example, in the early 2000s a young man aged twenty-three reported his recollection of an experience he had at age five or six in West Virginia; he did not specify the area. I have corrected some of the grammar:

> It was a long time ago in West Virginia on a clear but breezy day. I was about five or six on this day me and my granny were going to pick raspberries. As we were heading towards

where the berries were I can't remember who looked up first. But when I looked up I saw these big birds that were flying from over the mount. There were about two or three of them I don't really know how big they were but trust me when I say they were big. They look like they could pick up me and my granny. But they just flew right over us and their shadows huge too. They flew across the river towards the other mountains. The birds were black with some brown but mostly black. I told my mom but she says they were chicken hawks. But me and my granny know what we saw and they were not chicken hawks they were just too big. I am now 23 and me and my granny still remember. I am sure other people have seen these birds but have no evidence. Maybe someday someone will have a great picture or even better video of these birds. But until then the only thing we have is these stories. Sorry I only wish I had it on video.

I attempted to locate the author of this story but was unable to make contact with him. Of course to a child, a big bird might seem far more enormous than to an adult. As the author says, we have only stories.

An Elusive Photo of a Giant Winged Creature

One supposed photo of a flying monster has never been found—if it ever existed in the first place. Reports of the photo have circulated for decades, with many people claiming memories of having seen it in print in either magazines or books.

The hunt for the photo originates with a story published on April 26, 1890, in the Tombstone, Arizona, *Epitaph* that said two hunters had shot down a giant flying reptile resembling an alligator. The head alone was eight feet long, and the animal had a wingspan of 160 feet. The ranchers had plans to skin it. The sheer size of this creature alone makes the story suspect, for it would have dwarfed even the known giants of the dinosaur era.

The article made no mention of a photo, but one associated with the tale surfaced about eighty years later.

The story of the winged reptile was revived in the 1930s, and in 1963 a writer with the pseudonym "Jack Pearl" (real name Jacques Bain Pearl) claimed that in 1886 the *Epitaph* had published the photo of a giant bird, not a reptile, killed by two prospectors and nailed to a barn wall. The wingspan was thirty-six feet. Six men stood in front of the bird with their arms outstretched one-to-one to show the size.

No one has ever been able to find the photo, though many people, including Fortean researchers, have reported seeing it. Ivan T. Sanderson, a famous Fortean and naturalist, said he possessed a photostatic copy of it, which he loaned to two friends in 1966. They never returned it, and of course that was the only copy Sanderson had. (If true, one wonders why an astute researcher such as Sanderson would lend out such an important piece of evidence, even to friends, and especially without duplicating it. But stories of lent evidence that mysteriously disappears are legion in the paranormal.)

Even John A. Keel said in the 1990s that he had seen the elusive photo, but could provide no details.

In the early 2000s, Mark Chorvinsky, the publisher of *Strange Magazine*, initiated a long investigation of the thunderbird mystery, including the existence of the alleged photo. The investigation remained unfinished at the time of his death in 2005, but Chorvinsky did publish extensively on his findings and thought that the original article was an editorial prank characteristic of the nineteenth century. Others have thought the same. He found no evidence of a photo.

According to Chorvinsky, Pearl's source of information about the alleged photos probably was H. M. Cranmer, who lived in Pennsylvania and sent letters to *FATE* magazine about thunderbird sightings in the state. He said the photograph was taken in 1900 when two prospectors brought a giant bird carcass into Tombstone and nailed it to the wall of the *Epitaph*. Although Cranmer never said he saw the photo or owned a copy of it, others said he had a copy of it hanging in his living room, but it was destroyed in a fire that also took Cranmer's life. And so it goes once again with the disappearing evidence.

Chorvinsky's investigation inspired a number of hoaxed thunderbird photos, not only the "lost" *Epitaph* photo but others showing cowboys and even Civil War soldiers standing over downed pterodactyls. Numerous hoaxed "lost thunderbird" photos have appeared on the Internet.

Controversial, nonexistent, and hoaxed photos are a hazard in cryptozoology as well as the paranormal. Sometimes intriguing hard evidence is captured, as was the case during the 1977 Illinois wave of monster bird sightings. On July 30, 1977, an alleged thunderbird was filmed flying over Lake Shelby, Illinois, by a former Marine, John Huffer, who was out fishing with his son. Huffer and his son spotted two strange birds sitting in a tree and scared them with a blast of the boat horn. Huffer filmed one of them as it flew and landed in different trees. The film shows a large, dark bird, which the "experts" say is a turkey vulture. Huffer disagreed, pointing out the difference in shape and coloring; the unknown bird had no red ring around the neck, and its head and legs were shaped differently than those of a turkey vulture. Still, the film was not taken as serious evidence of a thunderbird or other mystery bird.

Photos of big birds are posted on the Internet from time to time as "possible" thunderbirds, but do not show enough detail to rule out ordinary, known birds. Photos that are not easy to explain away are still dismissed by "experts" and skeptics.

Conclusions

Like other mysterious creatures, monster birds may not live in our world, but in another dimension. Their appearances often come in waves of sightings in particular geographic areas, similar to waves of UFO activity, Bigfoot sightings, and other apparent supernatural "outbreaks." Waves of mysterious phenomena of all sorts may occur when doorways between dimensions pop open. For a period of time, lasting from a few days to weeks to even months, all manner of strange things may be experienced and seen. The rash of big bird sightings over Illinois in 1977 might be explained as an interdimensional opening. Suddenly, giant birds are in the skies. Just as mysteriously, sightings stop.

The story of the West Virginia 1895 mini-wave, only five years after the probably fictitious Tombstone terror, raises questions about authenticity, but at least some elements of the Addison story are hard to dismiss, in light of the Illinois and Pennsylvania reports. The 1895 West Virginia attacks and sightings may have been part of a larger wave that included the 1897 mystery airship sightings. A dirigible-like craft was seen over much of the American West and Midwest, and reached the Ohio River Valley. The airship wave may actually have started in 1896, with sightings reported in California. During 1897, airships sightings moved eastward across the continent. Some witnesses said the craft landed and odd-looking but humanoid beings got out and conversed with stunned humans. In Kentucky, they asked a farmer for food, and he cooked them egg sandwiches and pancakes. They told him they were from "a long way." They told another person they were from Mars. The full story digresses from our monsters investigations, but it is significant that various strange things were flying around in the skies all over America from 1895 to 1897. When a doorway opens, different phenomena may come through, and some of it may be of a shape-shifting nature.

As mentioned earlier, displacements of time must be considered as an explanation for some sightings, especially in the cases of creatures that strongly resemble extinct species. For example, the Clenedin "teratorn" might be such as case, in which a living creature from the past becomes temporarily displaced in time and space to appear in the present.

The Clenedin creature was feeding on what appeared to be roadkill. When it took off, perhaps it vanished back into its own time, which if so would present intriguing questions concerning the contamination of time periods. If it returned to our world as it was millions of years ago, then it took something from the present with it, which would have been digested and excreted in an ancient world.

As researchers of mysterious creatures and the paranormal know, labeling a creature is often tricky. Descriptions of varying creatures bleed together. The paranormal is a fluid, constantly morphing landscape. As we shall see, thunderbirds, big owls, and other unknown monster birds in West Virginia are entangled in accounts of flying humanoids and the state's most famous monster of all, Mothman.

Mothman

oint Pleasant seems on the surface an idyllic little town at the confluence of the Kanawha and Ohio Rivers. The scenery is spectacular and the surrounding countryside is quintessential bucolic. True, Point Pleasant has seen far better and more prosperous days, like many once-bustling towns lining the country's major riverways.

Underneath Point Pleasant lies a supernatural reality. Nearly everyone in town has at least one story to tell about a spooky encounter with a ghost or unknown creature or mystery lights in the sky. In the mid-1960s, the supernatural underbelly of Point exploded like a volcano, spewing forth creatures, aliens, spaceships, ghosts, poltergeists, Men in Black, giant birds, and other phenomena—and one of the most famous creatures now in the world: Mothman.

More than forty years on, residents and investigators alike still shake their heads and ask, "What on earth happened in Point Pleasant and, more than that, *why*?"

There are precious few answers to either question.

For thirteen months from 1966 to 1967, the Mid-Ohio River Valley was gripped by an onslaught of bizarre sightings and events. Point Pleasant was at the epicenter. The cast of characters came straight out of the *Twilight Zone*, and the star of the show was a huge, gray humanoid with wings, no marked head, and glowing red eyes set straight into what on a person would be the shoulder blades. Christened "Mothman"—a bit of a misnomer for it had no resemblance to a moth—the creature could rise up in the air like a helicopter, without flapping its wings, and fly at high speeds, with or without flapping its wings, even though the sound of wing flapping was sometimes heard. Witnesses were terrified and wanna-be witnesses flocked to areas where the entity had been spotted, in hopes of catching a glimpse. Some were armed, intent on capturing it dead or alive. But Mothman eluded them as mysteriously as it manifested, leaving behind not a speck of convincing hard evidence. Since the bizarre wave, Mothman sightings have been reported all over the world.

The most thorough investigation of the saga was conducted by John A. Keel, who participated in the unfolding of events during the wave—and who later had some alarming ideas of his own for explanations.

The First Encounter at Point Pleasant

The evening of November 15, 1966, was cold, clear, and crisp. Two young married couples who lived in Point Pleasant were out on a lark in the desolate TNT area, located on the Ohio River off Route 62 about six miles north of town. The TNT plant, officially known as the West Virginia Ordnance Works, was constructed as a munitions manufacturing site in 1942. The facility originally covered 8,323 acres. From 1942 to 1945, some 720,000 tons of TNT were produced each day there. The TNT was stored in bunkers called igloos, all built above ground. Underneath was a honeycomb of tunnels. The production led to significant ground and water contamination. After the war, the facility was abandoned and portions of it were sold off.

In 1966, the spooky plant was a favorite with couples who liked to park and neck. On this night, Roger and Linda Scarberry and Steve and Mary Mallette were out looking for friends and "chasing parkers," as Linda Scarberry related, much later in an exclusive interview with Donnie Sergent Jr. Roger was driving in his 1957 Chevrolet.

They made the rounds through the ghostly igloos without success and headed back to the unlocked gate at the old generator plant. They went over a small rise in the road, and the car headlights caught something that made Roger slam on the brakes.

Illuminated in front of them was a slender but muscular man-like creature, six to seven feet tall, with huge round red eyes, wings, and large hands. It had no definable head. The circular eyes looked more like they sprouted from the shoulders. The eyes, about two inches in diameter and about six to eight inches apart, stared at them with hypnotic intensity.

The creature was gray, or as Linda described much later, flesh-colored with ashen wings. One of its wings appeared to be caught in a guide wire near the road, and it pulled at the wing with its hands. Later, Linda thought the creature was frightened, but in the heat of the moment it was the occupants of the car who erupted in fear and panic. While they screamed, the creature wiggled its wing free and wobbled with an odd shuffling gait into the generator plant through an open, broken door.

Roger hit the gas and tore out of the gate onto the road, heading for Route 62 back to town. Suddenly, the creature was in sight again, standing on a little hill, as though it had instantly teleported itself. The car headlights struck it again, and it spread its ten-foot wings and took off straight into the air. It began following the car, matching its speed. Roger pressed the gas pedal down harder and harder until they were flying along Route 62 at 100 to 105 miles per hour. The creature effortlessly kept up, banging down on the roof of the car two or three times as they fled. It made a high-pitched squeaking noise like a mouse. (Reports differ as to whether the creature flapped its wing or not.)

Somehow they careened down the road and its dangerous curves without mishap. As they grew closer to the bright night lights of town, the creature peeled off. They saw it once again crouched on the Ohio River floodwall, its legs and wings tucked in.

Roger drove to the Dairyland and they tried to calm down and decide what to do. They could not agree on whether or not to report the creature to police, and they argued over whether or not they would be labeled crazy or drunk or both. A decision was made to return to the TNT area, but partway back they decided against it. When they turned back around they saw the body of a large dead dog by the side of the road. According to one of the witnesses, the winged creature jumped out at them as they passed the dog, went over the top of the car, and went through the field on the other side.

Back in town, the couples decided to notify the police and told their story to Deputy Millard Halstead. Seeing their genuine fright, Halstead took them seriously. He got in his patrol car and the two vehicles went back to the TNT area. The body of the dog was missing. There was no sign of the red-eyed monster, but when Millard turned on his police radio a strange garbled sound screeched out at high volume, as though someone were playing a tape recorder at fast-forward speed. Little did they know it, but this was the first of many manifestations of odd phenomenon to strike.

Linda and Roger were so rattled that they stayed up all night with the lights on. For a long time, Linda had trouble sleeping at night. The next day, the couples went back during daylight and found some odd-looking tracks resembling "two horseshoes put together" but smooth.

Also the next day, Sheriff George Johnson thought the incident warranted a press conference. The Scarberrys and Mallettes made themselves available for interviews. One of the reporters was Mary Hyre, who wrote a popular column for the *Athens Messenger* (in Athens, Ohio) called "Where Waters Mingle." Hyre sent her story to the Associated Press wire service. The Mason County "Bird" became instantly famous. Some anonymous editor or headline writer named it "Mothman" as a takeoff on the then-popular and campy television show, *Batman*.

Within two days, hundreds of cars full of eager people swarmed out to the TNT area and the nearby McClintic Wildlife Sanctuary at night in hopes of seeing Mothman. The atmosphere was like a supernatural party or picnic. Worried police estimated that every carful of people had at least one gun.

The debunkers were quick to jump in the fray, and the media were happy to oblige. One report claimed that the monster was nothing more than huge gas-filled balloons released by students doing air-current experiments. The debunker who got the most ink was Dr. Robert Smith, an associate professor of biology at West Virginia University, who said the creature had to be a sandhill crane, which stands four to six feet tall, has a large wingspan, and red feathers around its eyes. Never mind that the sandhill crane was a rarity in West Virginia, or that its overall shape bore no resemblance to the humanoid creature described by witnesses. Other explanations were that it was a shitepoke, which is a type of heron, and even a creature that flew down from the moon.

As feared, the original witnesses were ridiculed and accused of being drunk or on drugs. Point Pleasant is a religious community, but not a single minister called them to offer counseling. One minister laughed at them, Linda Scarberry said, and commented that the Devil had been run out of their church and that was the creature they saw. The Scarberrys were plagued at home by weird sounds at night, beeping noises, and something like a tape recorder being played at high speed. The noises became so disturbing that they left their trailer home and moved into the basement of Linda's parents.

More Sightings

Meanwhile, more people reported encounters with Mothman. One of the most terrifying of them happened on the night of November 16, just barely twenty-four hours after the Scarberrys and Mallettes had the fright of their lives. Marcella Bennett, her-two-year-old daughter Tina, and her brother Raymond Wamsley and his wife Cathy had decided to visit family members who lived near the TNT area. They had read about the strange being in the newspaper, and they even thought it might be fun to go out and look for it. They paid a visit at the home of a sister and brother-in-law and decided to depart around 9 P.M. They walked out to the car,

Marcella in the lead, holding a cigarette and her car keys and cradling little Tina in her arm.

Raymond was the first to see the creature, coming toward them out of the sky. Brilliant lights filled the area. Marcella kept on walking toward the car, oblivious to Raymond's shouts to stop and return to the house. She started to unlock the passenger door, and as she looked down, she saw a man's legs that looked like they were covered with gray feathers. She did not see any feet. Like a slow-motion horror film, she pulled her eyes up. Standing only a few feet away from her was a giant man-bird, its head sunken into the shoulder area and tilted to one side. She saw no red eyes, but later said she might have been too frightened to notice.

Marcella thought her life was over. She had never before seen anything so monstrous. Raymond screamed at her to run. Marcella turned, took four steps, and fell down on top of Tina. She felt paralyzed. Another, distant part of her thought the creature would scoop her up by her back. She heard the sound of flapping wings.

Marcella was at last able to rise and stumble to the porch with her daughter. She was skinned, bruised, bleeding, and burned by having also fallen on top of her lit cigarette. They all hurried into the house, where the children inside were screaming and crying in panic. Raymond called the county sheriff's office. It took about fifteen to twenty minutes for deputies to arrive—while Mothman lurked outside the house causing more terror. It came up on the porch, pushed on the door, and looked in the windows.

But the creature was gone by the time the deputies got there. The officers searched the area and found nothing.

Marcella was so traumatized that she could not sleep. Somehow, she felt the creature now had a link to her and would come back. After several days, she went to a hospital and was treated for shock. She was unable to drive at night. Once she had to go pick her husband up from work late at night. Suddenly, she was certain that "it" was in the backseat, and she nearly wrecked the car.

There were more sightings, night after night, on both sides of the Ohio River. They were all remarkably similar, of a tall bird-man with red eyes that rose straight up in the air like a helicopter.

On November 27, eighteen-year-old Connie Jo Carpenter saw the manlike "awful looking creature" flying toward her car on Route 33 near New Haven at about 10:30 P.M. In St. Albans, about forty miles south of Point Pleasant, two girls saw a flying creature with "big red pop-eyes." Even pilots reported the creature. Five pilots at Gallipolis Airport said they saw a winged form at about three hundred feet elevation around 3 P.M. on December 4. It was traveling at about seventy miles per hours without flapping its wings. This creature seemed to have a long neck, and it turned its head from side to side.

Many of the Mothman sightings were in the vicinity of the TNT. Every night, cars of armed hunters and thrill-seekers continued to pour through the area. Another major hot spot was the Chief Cornstalk Hunting Grounds (now the Chief Cornstalk Wildlife Management Area), 11,772 acres near Gallipolis Ferry, West Virginia, across the Kanawha River from Point Pleasant.

Though dozens and dozens of sightings were reported, Keel documented twenty-six that he considered to be the best and most responsible; one was from Mississippi on September 1, 1966, in which a flying humanoid was seen at low altitude in the vicinity of the town of Scott.

After the big news broke about Mothman, others came forward with accounts of earlier sightings. On November 1, National Guardsmen at the armory near Camp Conley Road in Point Pleasant saw a brown humanoid figure perched in a tree. On November 12, five men preparing a gravesite for a burial near Clendenin saw something that looked like a brown man with wings lift off from the trees nearby. On November 14, glowing red eyes were reported in Salem, West Virginia.

Birdman and Other Weird Birds

Complicating the sightings of Mothman were reports of huge, unusual birds on both sides of the Ohio River. One of the creatures was Birdman, an owl-human thing that favored lonely creeks in Kanawha, Roane, Mason, Jackson, Wood, and Braxton Counties.

Birdman has shiny, reddish feathers, a humanlike head, and a wingspan of about twelve feet.

Appalachian folklorist James Gay Jones documented a wave of Birdman sightings around the turn of the twentieth century. The huge man-bird with reddish feathers that glistened in the sunlight made appearances just before or after tragic events in Point Pleasant. Around World War I, the creature was seen flying over Looneyville, up Johnson Creek and down Gabe in Roane County, and down the Elk Valley into the Kanawha, Jones said. Parents forbade their small children to play outside. Another wave centered along the Ohio River took place after World War II in the late 1940s. In the latter wave, some witnesses said Birdman chased them in their cars as they drove in the vicinity of the Ohio River in Mason, Jackson, and Wood Counties.

When the Mothman wave commenced, Birdman sightings were mixed with Mothman reports, and may have created some confusion. Some sightings were of giant birds. Thomas Ury, a resident of Point Pleasant, was driving on Route 62 just north of the TNT plant on November 25 at about 7:15 A.M. when he saw a huge, grayish bird in the air that zeroed in on his vehicle for a few minutes. It circled the car, drawing closer and closer. Ury gauged it to have a wingspan of about ten to twelve feet.

Ury was not the only person seeing odd birds instead of winged humanoids. Strange birds were reported as far away as Pennsylvania and up to seventy miles away in Ohio.

UFOs, Aliens, and High Strangeness

Mothman alone would be enough for the record books of mysterious creatures, but almost immediately—and even preceding the Scarberry-Mallette encounter—area residents were subjected to more phenomena. In fact, the Mid-Ohio Valley became the focal point of a full-blown "high strangeness" wave, with Point Pleasant at the center. *High strangeness* is a term used in ufology to describe the secondary phenomena that often accompany sightings and encounters with alien lights, craft, and beings. Witnesses, already disoriented from their primary events, become even further disoriented in a landscape of poltergeist activity, apparitions, Men in Black visits, odd phone calls, electrical disturbances, nightmares, Shadow People, missing and mutilated animals, and more.* All of those things happened during the entire run of the Mothman wave. People who actually saw Mothman suffered more high strangeness than others. It was as though they were now on some strange "radar" targeted for monitoring. Others plagued by high strangeness included researchers, investigators, and persons who took strong interest in penetrating the mystery.

UFO activity began prior to Mothman's first known appearance. The most dramatic case to hit the headlines was Woodrow Derenberger's meeting with an alien named Indrid Cold. The initial incident occurred on November 2 on Interstate 77 outside of Parkersburg, at about 7 P.M. Derenberger was heading home to Mineral Wells, south of Parkersburg, from his job as a shoe salesman in Clarksburg.

A craft materialized and landed on the interstate, forcing him to stop. A tall, slim manlike entity emerged, came to his car, and conversed with him telepathically. Indrid Cold explained his people meant no harm—and that he would be in further contact.

Derenberger's encounters with Cold resumed two nights later, when the alien came to his home. When news got out, Derenberger was an instant celebrity, and people camped out at his home in hopes of catching sight of a "real" extraterrestrial. Cold told Woody that he was from a planet named Lanulos in the constellation Ganymede. There is no such constellation, at least in our reality. But Derenberger got launched into an alternate reality that ultimately isolated and alienated him from others, including his own family.

---

*Men in Black are mysterious men, dressed in black clothing and usually driving black cars, who harass UFO witnesses and threaten them not to divulge what they saw. Shadow People are solid black, featureless silhouettes of tall men in coats and sometimes hats, who appear in bedrooms at night and terrify people. They are often linked to ET and UFO activity.

The most famous missing animal of the Mothman wave was Bandit, a German shepherd belonging to Newell Partridge near Salem. On the night of November 14, Bandit became agitated, and the Partridge home was filled with electrical disturbances and odd sounds. Partridge went outside to see why the dog was howling, and shined his flashlight into the darkness. The light picked up two odd eyes that did not seem to be animal eyes. Bandit took off and was never seen again. The next day, Partridge found the dog's tracks by the barn, as though it had chased something in circles.

Was the dead dog seen the next night by the Scarberrys and Mallettes the body of Bandit? The carcass mysteriously disappeared soon after it was seen.

John A. Keel spent a great deal of time in Point Pleasant during the wave, documenting the sightings and high strangeness and having some of his own weird experiences as well. Once he checked into a motel without a reservation—and found a phone message waiting for him. He teamed up with Mary Hyre, and the two went out at night to watch the strange lights in the sky, especially near Gallipolis Ferry. He was in frequent contact with Ivan T. Sanderson and Gray Barker.

Keel received phone calls from entities claiming to be aliens, who had prophecies about world events and disasters that were going to happen. Even after returning to New York City, he was fed messages of prophecies and predictions from sources all over the country. One message predicted a power failure all over the country on the night of December 15, 1967.

The date was significant, but not for a power failure. On that evening at about 5 P.M.—the coldest day of the entire year—a traffic jam occurred on the Silver Bridge spanning the Ohio River at Point Pleasant. The bridge was loaded with cars and trucks, many full of Christmas shoppers. Traffic was at a standstill, apparently because of a faulty stoplight. Suddenly an I-beam on the suspension bridge failed and the structure started to sway and twist. It collapsed into the river, sending forty cars and seventeen trucks into the frigid, icy water. Forty-six people lost their lives, among them Marvin Wamsley, the teenaged nephew of Raymond and Cathy Wamsley.

Within an hour of the disaster, twelve UFOs were spotted over the TNT area. The emotional shock sent the entire community reeling. Nearly everyone in Point Pleasant was affected by the tragedy, losing either a relative or a friend, or knowing others who suffered losses.

Premonitions about the bridge collapsing, people drowning, and packages floating in the river had been experienced for months. Mary Hyre herself had a premonitory dream. Now, in the aftermath, some people tied the whole Mothman wave to the collapse. Mothman became a portent of doom.

The trauma seemed to shut off most of the paranormal activity, which dropped significantly in the wake of the collapse. Undoubtedly, many people simply did not have the emotional energy to lend to Mothman, but were consumed by grief and other grittier matters.

Today, people in Point Pleasant are divided over whether Mothman had anything to do with the bridge collapse.

Mothman Today

Mothman sightings still occur in the Mid-Ohio Valley, though none have excited the frenzy of the original wave. The TNT plant was torn down in the mid-1990s, but the igloos, long empty of chemicals and munitions, remained. Many of them were open and accessible. The grounds and igloos became favorites of Mothman hunters, who took photos and collected mysterious voices (electronic voice phenomena, or EVPs) on their recorders. Every trip I took to Point Pleasant included trekking through the igloos; however, I never had a sighting of anything mysterious.

In May 2010, some forgotten munitions in a tunnel beneath an igloo exploded, and the entire area was sealed off to traffic until further notice. All igloos were off limits until fall 2011, when access to several of them was reopened.

Keel's book was turned into a film in 2002, *The Mothman Prophecies*, starring Richard Gere as John Klein, based on Keel. The film was a disappointment to fans and the general audience alike. It took major departures from Keel's book and was so vague about what happened that anyone who did not already know about Mothman was still in the dark by the end of the film. Debra Messing played Mary, the wife of Klein; in real life, Keel was never married.

Nonetheless, the film reignited interest in Mothman. In 2002, the first Mothman Festival was held in Point Pleasant, organized by Jeff Wamsley and Carolin Harris, whose husband was one of the Silver Bridge victims. Keel was the star of the second festival, at which a giant statue of Mothman was dedicated on Guinn Street downtown. The event was so popular that it has continued as an annual event, with a street fair, haunted hayride through the TNT area, Miss Mothman beauty contest, film and documentary screenings, and lectures by researchers such as myself on a wide variety of topics; I have been a regular there since 2004. Wamsley also runs a Mothman Museum, which is open year-round.

The Meaning of Mothman

No one has ever been able to satisfactorily explain why Point Pleasant and a large area around it were literally turned upside down for about a year. Yet the question (and the possible answer) has a bearing on everything discussed in this book.

First, let's eliminate some popular and often-discussed explanations. One that still makes the rounds has been debunked: a curse on the land by an eighteenth-century Shawnee chief named Hokoleskwa, literally translated as "stalk of corn." Cornstalk, as he was known to the English, opposed settlement by the Europeans on Shawnee land. On October 10, 1774, Shawnee and Mingo warriors suffered a heavy defeat against Virginia militia in the Battle of Point Pleasant. Thereafter, perhaps seeing the handwriting on the wall, Cornstalk began working for peaceful cooperation with the white settlers.

In the fall of 1777, Cornstalk, his son Elinipsico, and two Shawnee made a diplomatic trip to Fort Randolph, now in Point Pleasant. On November 10, a militia man was killed by a band of unknown Indians. Enraged, the militia men took revenge and arrested Cornstalk, his son, and the other Shawnee, holding them prisoners at the fort. All of them were shot at point-blank range by militia men who burst into their cell. All four were killed.

Lore has it that Cornstalk leveled a curse on the land as he lay dying. "I came to the fort as your friend and you murdered me," the chief cried. "You have murdered by my side, my young son. . . . For this, may the curse of the Great Spirit rest upon this land. May it be blighted by nature. May it even be blighted in its hopes. May the strength of its peoples be paralyzed by the stain of our blood." Supposedly the land was cursed for two hundred years.

Recently, the curse was debunked as a fiction for an outdoor play written in the early twentieth century, presented at Point Pleasant. The theory makes sense. A man taken by surprise and shot multiple times at point-blank range and who was not killed instantly probably would not be able to muster much consciousness for anything in his final moments, let alone the dramatic pronouncement given above.

Other explanations are mutant creatures caused by the toxic chemicals at the TNT plant, and weird creatures created by someone's occult rituals. Both explanations fall far short of the bill and cannot possibly account for the wide range of everything that went on—and still goes on.

Linda Scarberry, who died in 2011, believed that Mothman was "sent" to take people's attention away from the UFO activity—perhaps as a decoy. But "who" did the sending, and from where? More likely, Mothman was one of many players on an alternate-reality stage.

Keel favored the "window" explanation: Point Pleasant happened to be at a place where a portal ripped open between dimensional realities. I favor that as well. In fact, the area may be in a permanent paranormal hot zone, with thin interdimensional boundaries that allow bleed-throughs on a frequent basis. For reasons we do not know, the 1966–1967 wave was a huge bleed-through. Supernatural phenomena still occur, but not to the great and dramatic extent of that wave.

Keel's investigations of the Mothman wave and other phenomena convinced him by 1967 that the entities called "extraterrestrials" were not from other planets, but from other dimensions. He soon coined a better term: "ultraterrestrial." His ideas did not set well with the conventional ufologists, but in the ensuing decades, they have proven their validity. More than anyone, Keel set the bar for evaluating and explaining everything paranormal, from ghosts and hauntings to UFOs and mysterious creatures, to entities and spirits of unknown origins. *Ultraterrestrial* is now used to describe virtually any unknown entity, not just ones related to UFOs.

In 1970, five years before his book *The Mothman Prophecies* was released, Keel published *UFOs: Operation Trojan Horse*, the first of several books in which he expanded on his ideas about the interconnections of all psychic phenomena. According to Keel, our reality and beliefs are manipulated by some unknown, nonhuman intelligence. Phenomena are generated to perpetuate certain belief systems. It's all a big phantasmagoria, a "Disneyland of the Gods," which may explain the bizarre nature of so much that is paranormal and why we never get solid answers or evidence. We humans have no control over the process, he said, and we can only wonder at what is the *real* agenda.

Keel, who died in 2009, remains controversial. When it comes to mysterious creatures, some investigators feel the creatures are a part of this reality, and will someday be found and perhaps captured. Others, including me, say Keel is right, or at least partially right: the mysterious creatures come from other dimensions, but we are not necessarily powerless puppets in a cosmic drama or comedy.

The Continuing Mystery

Mothman as a portent of doom became unshakeable, at least in part of the lore about the creature. Winged, flying humanoids spotted around the world are labeled Mothman, and whenever there is a catastrophic disaster, researchers scour for premonitory sightings. Keel made connections between Mothman and the *garuda*, a large man-bird in Buddhist and Hindu mythologies that protects against evil. Does that mean that it appears when evil is about to happen? The events happen, anyway, so where might be the protection?

Major disasters are sometimes preceded by UFO waves. Waves of mystery creature sightings accompany UFO waves. So, whenever we have a spate of sightings, should we brace for something bad, without knowing when and where it will happen? There seems to be little else we can do.

Strange things still occur in Point Pleasant. As of this writing I have not seen Mothman, but I have experienced apparitions, poltergeist phenomena, the recording of mystery voices, phone disturbances, and odd displacements of time. On one occasion, I saw what may have been the double of my friend John Frick, walking along a street in Point Pleasant, while John himself was actually in one of the igloos at the TNT site. John and his brother Tim have had numerous odd experiences during their ongoing Mothman research and in participating in the Mothman Festival as Men in Black.

Synchronistic events and six-degrees-of-separation connections relating Mothman to a host of global events, conspiracies, cults, mass murders, disasters, and other paranormal watershed events are explored by researchers, among them Andrew B. Colvin, a native of Charleston who now lives in Seattle. Colvin, an artist, photographer, and author, became interested in what might be a "Mothman Code" after the World Trade Center terrorist attacks on September 11, 2001. A West Virginia school friend had predicted such a disaster in 1967, saying that it would happen in 2001 and would be the start of World War III. The friend said he had been given the information by "space aliens" and a flying birdman.

Colvin delved into intense research, concluding that perhaps he was being an unwitting cipher for the Mothman Code to release information in a "cosmic setup" of some sort. Echoing Keel, he observed in his book *Mothman's Photographer II* (2007) that "Mothman presents electromagnetic mirrors to us, to see ourselves and other parts of the human matrix. Occasionally, a veil might be used. He/she/it observes our responses, and reports back to what seems like another part of the matrix."

Ultimately, those who have unexplained experiences have to arrive at their own truth. For some, the experience is "just one of those things," and for others, it has cosmic significance.

The Braxton County Monster

O n September 12, 1952, one of the strangest and most terrifying encounters with an unknown entity took place near Flatwoods, a small town in Braxton County. A group of boys playing outdoors were startled to see a brilliant light streak down from the sky, fly overhead, and appear to crash to earth on a nearby hill. Those who were brave enough to investigate found a crashed craft and a monstrous creature that could move by levitating off the ground. It seemed to be intelligent—and it defended itself against the humans with sickening gases and oil.

The "alien" was immediately seared into local folklore. The Braxton County Monster—also called the Flatwoods Monster, the Green Monster, and the Phantom of Flatwoods—became one of the most curious unexplained cases on record, intriguing ufologists, paranormal researchers, and media all over the world. Was the monster an extraterrestrial, an unknown creature, or a machine—or all of them mixed together in some weird hybrid? Why was it here? In the aftermath, "officials" from Washington came to Flatwoods to interview witnesses and collect their evidence, which was never seen again. The case was then buried by debunkers and ridiculing media.

Although the Braxton County Monster is usually described as a UFO or ET case, it can also be a "monster" case. Even considering the streaking light from the sky and a crashed craft, the entity may have come from another dimension, not outer space. The case has had a lasting impact on the area, for ever since then, almost any strange creature reported, no matter what its description, is likely to be labeled by the press as the Flatwoods Monster, Braxton County Monster, or Green Monster.

The Invasion of Flatwoods

On the night of September 12, 1952, a wave of UFO sightings occurred over a large portion of the eastern United States, including Pennsylvania, West Virginia, Virginia, Ohio, Tennessee, Maryland, and Washington, D.C. Blazing objects were seen hurtling through the skies, and many witnesses thought they were airplanes crashing in flames.

In Flatwoods, a group of ten boys were playing in a schoolyard, enjoying the Indian summer evening. They ranged in age from ten years to fourteen; the ages of three of them at the time are not known. They saw one of these fireballs soar overhead, with flames trailing behind it, before it came down at a nearby farm owned at the time by a man named Bailey Fisher. The boys ran to investigate. They passed by the home of two of the boys who were brothers, Edison May and Freddie May. Their excitement about a landed "flying saucer" caused their mother, Kathleen May, to join the hunt, as well as eighteen-year-old Eugene Lemon, who brought his dog. Five of the boys decided to go home. The other five, plus the two adults, went on to the crash site. By then it was about 7:40 P.M. and getting dark, so they took flashlights.

They found an object crashed into the earth and sticking out; it appeared to be pulsing in brightness. A strange sound like whining or hissing filled the air. There was a violet hue to the air. After their arrival, a mysterious foglike mist began to blanket the area. It had a nauseating, metallic smell and irritated their throats and lungs. The dog became agitated, began barking violently, and took off. It was later found back in town, where it had vomited on a house veranda. It died soon thereafter.

Back at the crash site, the boys and adults had yet to realize that the object had actually landed twice, first on the hilltop and then in the valley, and that something living had emerged from it. When they saw it, they at first thought that an animal was perched in a nearby tree, looking at them. Kathleen May shined her flashlight at it, and the entire group got a horrible shock. Instead of an animal, they saw a twelve-foot-tall figure with glowing eyes standing next to the tree. As soon as the flashlight beam hit it, the eyes shot out brilliant beams of light that illuminated the entire fog-filled area.

The creature seemed to be more of a machine, a metallic casing or suit—or perhaps a creature inside a suit. It was dark in color but seemed green to some of the witnesses, perhaps because the metallic-like surface reflected the green of the surrounding trees and bushes. It also glowed with light. The middle torso seemed like a cylinder, and the lower torso fanned out like a metallic apron of sorts. Where one might expect arms there were only two short antenna-like things sticking straight out. Its head was round and surrounded by a stiff cowl or helmet shaped like an ace of spades. The round eyes looked like portholes. It had no feet, but levitated about a foot off the ground and maneuvered around in this manner.

The creature glided close to Kathleen May, who felt a warm mist around it. Without warning, it squirted an oily substance all over her clothes. There seemed to be no immediate ill effect from the oil, but the nauseating mist continued to burn their throats. The creature left a trail of oil on the ground as it glided.

Suddenly the horror of it hit the witnesses, and all of them, adults and boys, fled back to town as fast as they could run. At the May-Lemon home (Kathleen and her boys lived in a house owned by her father, Joe Lemon), chaos erupted. The Mays and Lemon all had trouble breathing, and the boys were bruised and bleeding, probably from their pell-mell flight. Lemon vomited all night long. Kathleen's eyes were red and teary. Edison and Freddie required medical treatment for their damaged mouths and throats.

Around 8:15 P.M., Kathleen telephoned the sheriff's office to report their experience, and the sheriff in turn notified the state police. A state trooper telephoned the co-owner, publisher, and photojournalist for the *Braxton Democrat*, A. Lee Stewart Jr. Stewart jumped to join the investigation. He went to the May house and gathered a group of armed men, among them Eugene and Joe Lemon, and went out to the scene, but the monster was gone. Some of its sickening odor lingered behind. Sheriff Robert Carr, meanwhile, took two of his dogs to the area, but the dogs ran off howling into the fog. He gave up until morning. He found his clothing had been stained by some sort of oil.

The military was quick to become involved. The West Virginia National Guard was mobilized by the U.S. Air Force and sent to Flatwoods and also to Frametown, about nineteen miles away, where another fireball in the sky had been seen coming down. About thirty troops under the command of Capt. Dale Leavitt descended on the Flatwoods site by about 1:30 A.M. They were soon joined by more troops, with the assignment to look for a downed "airplane." They found nothing, even though some of them stayed all night. A few troops searched the area again in daylight.

Stewart also returned to the scene in early daylight and examined some thirty-foot-long skidmarks left in the grass. While he was studying the marks, his clothes were stained again by the mysterious oil. He found a small, odd piece of silvery metal that looked like dripped solder. He was the first person to break the story in the press.

The West Virginia media reported the UFO lights as meteorlike objects streaking across the sky, seen by numerous witnesses throughout a wide area. The story of the monster and how the first witnesses became faint and ill by something that looked like "Frankenstein" spread rapidly. By afternoon, Flatwoods was swarming with people looking for evidence and souvenirs. They picked up more bits of metal and pieces of a black plasticlike substance and found more traces of oil.

A Fright near Frametown

The monster sightings were by no means over. A young couple and their eighteen-month-old son encountered the creature near Frametown on September 13, terrifying them so badly that they didn't speak about it for years.

George and Edith Snitowsky, of Queens, New York, had traveled by car to Cincinnati, Ohio, to visit a relative. They were on their return trip, leisurely taking the secondary roads. Around 8 P.M. they entered Braxton County and traveled along what is now State Route 4. Between Gassaway and Frametown, their car died without warning. They could not restart the engine. While George tried to figure out the problem, the air around them filled with a sickening smell that seemed like a combination of ether and burnt sulfur. At first George thought the car engine might be burning, but that was not the source. The smell agitated their baby, who began crying.

As darkness settled in, George was in a quandary. Frametown, the nearest town, was about twelve miles away, too far away for a practical walk. Besides, he was reluctant to leave his wife and infant alone in the car. Suddenly a blinding violet light shot out of the woods. George opened a window, and the interior of the car filled with a choking, nauseating mist. Despite the smell, he got out to investigate, retching violently.

About two hundred to three hundred yards away was a luminescent spheroid that looked like a giant frosted street lamp. It floated in the air and moved back and forth. George walked closer, still sick. He began to feel hot, and then felt a sensation like low-grade electric shock course through his body. Now frightened, he turned to hurry back to the car, but his legs turned rubbery and he fell repeatedly.

Then he heard Edith scream. It was a blood-curdling scream, like a banshee. He lurched back to the car, where he saw a huge figure illuminated in the light from the spheroid. It was about eight to nine feet tall and shaped like a man but with a reptilian head. It had shoulders, a weirdly bloated body, and a lower torso that seemed to be a solid mass of some sort.

George scrambled into the car and pushed his wife and child onto the floor. He grabbed a knife out of the glove compartment. The creature moved closer until it was directly in front of the car. It reached out a spindly arm that ended in a soft, bisected fork of "fingers" and ran it across the windshield and hood, as though it was examining the car. Then it turned and glided into the woods, disappearing from sight. Within a few minutes, a globe of light rose slowly above the trees and moved into the sky, suddenly shooting away in a trail of brilliant light.

Badly shaken, George tried the ignition again, and this time the car started without a problem. They drove until they reached a truck stop diner, probably near Sutton, and went inside to compose themselves. They resolved not to talk about what happened. They then found a hotel and spent the night. The next morning, George found a forked discoloration on the hood of his car where the entity had touched it. The metal looked like it had been singed.

Bashful Billy

On September 15, residents of Wheeling sent up a hue and cry with calls to the police department about sightings of a monster near the Vineyard Hill Housing Development near Oglebay Park. The media dubbed the creature a "fugitive from fairyland," which flew in on a flying saucer. It left before anyone actually saw it, thus earning the nickname "Bashful Billy." All of the calls to police, apparently, were second-hand reports.

However, there were reports of a body of a badly burned woman found at Vineyard Hill, with no further details provided. Was it really a woman—or a dead alien?

The Aftermath

The original witnesses at Flatwoods were subject to intense media scrutiny. Men who said they were from "the government" in Washington came and interviewed them and took away their oil-stained clothing, bits of metal and plastic, and other pieces of evidence. None of it was ever returned.

Descriptions of the monster reported in the media became distorted. The creature had "bulging eyes," clawed hands, and was green with a "blood-red face." It wore a "monk-like" robe or tunic. It was half man and half dragon, and it breathed fire. It was a "Frankenstein monster with B.O." Police were quoted dismissing the monster as the product of "mass hysteria."

The original witnesses were invited to be interviewed by the press and to appear on television. They were portrayed as ignorant country folk whose imaginations had run away with them and who had been "scared out of their wits." The *Charleston Daily Mail* reported on September 15 that the monster was nothing more than the combination of an airplane warning beacon and a flashing meteor reflecting on the trunk of a dead tree.

On September 23, the *Charleston Gazette* ran an interview with a "local insurance man and amateur astronomer" who insisted that the monster was an illusion created by gases from a meteor. Earl Stephens of Belle said that fireballs originate from an electrical discharge in the earth's outer atmosphere and give off sulfur gases:

> Stephens said one of the parties apparently flashed the light on the gas ball just the instant before it disintegrated into thin air. The reflection of the light on the gases gave it the shape the people described, he said. . . .
>
> Stephens offered his theory to The Gazette in the interest of what he termed "attempting to erase the fear of supernatural beings from the minds of the people."

On October 9, the *Charleston Daily Mail* gave considerable space to a woman identified as "Aunt Rebecca Frame," age ninety, who insisted that the Braxton Monster was "pure silliness" and was mistaken for a snake, which "grow big up there."

With such convoluted, ludicrous explanations as above, ordinary citizens might have more to fear from the so-called "experts" than from any supernatural beings.

Kathleen May said she received a letter from Washington, D.C. about a month after the incident informing her that the object was an experimental military craft designed for lunar travel, and that four of them had appeared in the skies on the night of the monster encounter. This seemed to be corroborated by the publication of an article about moon rockets in *Collier's* magazine at the same time as the arrival of the letter.

The Flatwoods case attracted the attention of leading UFO researchers of the time, among them retired Maj. Donald E. Keyhoe, Ivan T. Sanderson, and Gray Barker, who conducted their own interviews. Sanderson concluded that the case was real, and that the monster was from somewhere else, not earth. Keyhoe commented that this was the weirdest of all saucer stories and had dangerous implications because of its "fearsome creature intelligent enough to build and control space ships." To the public and media, however, the story was more of a carnival sideshow. After a flurry of attention, the case fell into the backwaters.

Inevitably, claims of hoaxing surfaced. Whenever a major story breaks in the paranormal, with eyewitness accounts or photos of mysterious entities, it is not unusual for someone to come forward and claim to have hoaxed the whole thing. Sometimes hoax claims tie investigators up in knots. Other times the claims do not hold up and probably are made by people trying to grab a bit of the spotlight or have a joke on those who take the cases seriously.

In 1977, reporter Adrian Gwin of the *Charleston Daily Mail* revisited the Braxton County Monster case and reported that the newspaper had been contacted "recently" (presumably close to the publication of the article) by a former resident of West Virginia who claimed responsibility for hoaxing the monster. Bill Steorts, formerly of St. Albans and Sutton, and at the time of his writing a resident of West Palm Beach, Florida, said that on the night of September 12, 1952, he and A. Lee Stewart Jr. were driving from

Heaters to Sutton when they ran out of gas. Steorts said in a letter to the paper:

> We noticed a disturbance across the road and went to investigate.
>
> There were some small children all stirred up. Having a sawed-off 12-gauge in the car, we went on the hill to see what was going on. The kids had been playing in a pasture field and some of Bailey Fisher's cows were in nearby woods. Seeing that nothing had happened, we went on to Sutton.
>
> Being slightly intoxicated, we fabricated the story of the Braxton County Monster. We called the Gazette from the Braxton Democrat office. Stewart's dad owned the newspaper at the time.
>
> The skid marks were made by Bailey's old Ford Tractor spinning its wheels—the grease was raked from under the tractor by tall grass.
>
> We drew the artist's picture of the monster.
>
> From there it just mushroomed. Kathleen May and her children went to New York on a TV show. Scientists from all over came to investigate. We sat back and laughed. My father knew what we boys were doing but his store was doing a booming business from the tourist trade.

As is often the case in hoax claims, no substantiation was offered, just the claim itself. Oddly, many people will believe a claim such as this despite the overwhelming evidence to the contrary. It's as though human beings are uncomfortable with evidence of unknown creatures in our midst and thus will grab at any straw to convince themselves otherwise.

Sometimes reports were treated in jest, such as a "lighter side" account from 1961 in a United Press International story out of Charleston. The story concerned the "Marion monster" and said in part:

This past summer, a "monster" appeared again—this time in Marion County. Some people in the Bunner's ridge area were convinced that the old Braxton monster had returned to plague them. One boy was so terrified when he saw the "thing" that he dived headfirst through a plate glass window of a barber shop at Worthington.

The Marion "monster" also disappeared as quickly as he had appeared. But some people in that area said it wasn't so mysterious, that sponsors of a community fair dressed somebody up to look like a monster as a promotion stunt. The fair managers never admitted it, though.

A Search for the Truth

In 1990, Frank C. Feschino Jr., an artist and paranormal researcher, became interested in the Flatwoods case while visiting relatives in Braxton County. Riveted, he began an investigation that consumed much of his life for the next decade. Feschino tracked down original eyewitnesses, delved into media reports and government documents, and interviewed military and government sources. He published his findings in 2004 in his book *The Braxton County Monster: The Cover-Up of the Flatwoods Monster Revealed*, revised in 2007. The summary I have given of this case is based on his well-researched investigation.

Feschino had a much different account from A. Lee Stewart Jr., whom he located for an interview. Stewart had left West Virginia in 1958—and left the Braxton County Monster story behind him as well. He was, said Feschino, shocked at how he had been "grossly misquoted and portrayed by previous reporters and writers."

According to Stewart, after getting the call from state trooper Ted Tribett at about 9 P.M., he headed out to the May home. En route he passed the Steorts' store, where Bill and his father were still working, and picked up Bill to take along. At the May home, they found panic and turmoil. Stewart recruited a group to investigate; they were armed with a 12-gauge automatic shotgun and handguns. At the site, they found the skidmarks, noted the lingering foul odor, but found no monster. They returned to the May home, where Stewart talked more with the witnesses. Then he took Bill Steorts home and went back to his office. He called a friend who had a reel-to-reel tape recorder that he wanted to borrow to interview the witnesses on record, which he intended to do the next day. He contacted his attorney, Olin Berry, to ask advice on breaking the story. He went to Berry's home, and Berry placed a call to the *Charleton Gazette* at about 2 A.M., explaining to the paper that Stewart should be credited with breaking the story.

Sifting through conflicting accounts is one of the most difficult tasks of ascertaining what really happens in entity contact cases. Feschino found enough corroborating accounts and evidence to make a number of conclusions: The "meteors" that flashed through the skies in September 1952 were actually sixteen alien craft in groups of four. They appeared over the Gulf of Mexico, where mock war-game exercises were taking place. Feschino speculates that perhaps the aliens thought the games were real war and were monitoring them. Their crafts were detected and were pursued by Air Force fighter jets, which engaged them in combat. One of the alien craft was damaged and landed at Flatwoods.

The marooned creature that was seen by witnesses was encased in a metallic suit. On the second night, it had moved to the Frametown area and was seen by the Snitowskys partially out of its suit. It evidently was rescued and escaped. Another damaged craft crashed at Wheeling; the creature may have been killed and its body recovered by authorities, who substituted a "burned woman corpse" cover story to deflect attention. Government officials quickly moved to collect evidence, discredit the witnesses, and dismiss the entire affair.

In his foreword and epilogue to Feschino's book, ufologist Stanton T. Friedman notes that the evidence adds up to a cover-up of a "truly outstanding and important event."

I have met Frank Feschino Jr. on several occasions and have discussed the case with him. In March 2011, I had another opportunity to get an update from him. He has collected more accounts from people who witnessed the fireballs in the sky and also had sightings of creatures in the woods; there seemed to have been more than one entity per craft. The witnesses remained silent for years. "They don't talk about it," Feschino told me. "They learned their lesson from Flatwoods," referring to the humiliating treatment of the primary witnesses.

One question he had during his investigation was why did the marooned entity seen near Frametown remain in the lower portion of its "suit," rather than jettison it in order to improve its odds of hiding? The suit was huge and ungainly, about four to five feet wide, and the entity plus suit must have weighed 350 to 400 pounds, quite a hefty package to levitate off the ground. The reason, he believes, is that the entity had no legs. Its lower portion was coiled inside like a snake. Its exposed head was reptilian in features, according to George Snitowsky.

Feschino said that Gray Barker, Ivan T. Sanderson, and an assistant to Sanderson went to a crash site at Sugar Creek. There they saw trees ripped down and a big indentation and divots in the earth. They also found pieces of a coiled substance, which were sent to the Monsanto chemical company for analysis. When the substance was put in water, it uncoiled. It resembled a giant piece of snakeskin, but made out of a harder substance like turtle shell.

Flatwoods Today

Several festivals have been held in Flatwoods commemorating the anniversary of the 1952 case, but the festivals have not achieved the popularity of the Mothman Festival held further south in Point Pleasant.

Folks in the Flatwoods area today say there is a lingering atmosphere of fear and dread. The valley is full of dead trees and seemingly barren dirt, with skimpy vegetation and a queer absence of much wildlife. Reports of mysterious creatures lurking about include Bigfoot-like forms and a large, hairy "werewolf" that, though rarely seen, can be heard making blood-chilling howls. The history of mystery creatures in Braxton County is long and precedes the 1952 case. As I mentioned at the beginning, the media has dubbed subsequent sightings of creatures as the Braxton County Monster, although they probably have no connection to the 1952 case.

Who or what really invaded our reality in September 1952? Will the full truth ever be known about the Braxton County Monster? As Kathleen May told Feschino, "The government just tells you what they want you to believe."

The Yayho: West Virginia's Bigfoot

Longtime mountain residents in certain parts of West Virginia know them as Yayhos or Yahoos (yay-hoos): giant, hairy apemen that live in the dense forests, make blood-curdling screams, throw stones, bang big sticks on trees, follow people with heavy footsteps, tear animals apart—and scare the living daylights out of people. Sightings and encounters have occurred for generations. Hunts and expeditions have been mounted to capture one, or at least capture convincing proof of one. But the Yayhos, like others of their kind all over the world known as Bigfoot and numerous other names, remain just out of reach.

The hundreds of reported sightings of Bigfoot throughout West Virginia are probably just a fraction of the activity that takes place. Systematic efforts to document and collect reports have been in effect for only a decade or two, and many people who encounter Bigfoot say nothing, perhaps out of fear of ridicule.

Despite the lack of hard proof, the anecdotal evidence is hard to ignore. Camp, hike, hunt, or fish in the wilderness, or drive along the back country roads, and surprises may await you, day or night. There are huge dwellers in the wild that are not human and not animal. They are very intelligent, and their reactions to humans run the gamut from curiosity to fear to hostility and aggression.

On the night of June 30, 2007, a man named Nick (a pseudo-nym I have given the anonymous witness) left a family campsite near the Cranberry River in the Monongahela National Forest to head home. He decided to take a shortcut on backroads through Cranberry Ridge that would lead him out to Camden. Nick had grown up in the mountains and knew the roads and terrain well. Around midnight, he was near the county line between Nicholas and Webster Counties. Suddenly, a huge form loomed out of the darkness—a massive creature standing in the middle of the road.

At first Nick thought it was "some idiot in a monkey suit." It was man-ape in appearance, about six feet tall, and covered com-pletely in reddish-brown fur. Even its bare feet were hairy. Nick honked his horn and the creature took off at a fast run in long strides. It turned to look at him with an ape-like face. At that point, Nick realized it was no human. The creature ran up a hill in front of Nick, tore through some elderberry bushes, and disap-peared down the mountain.

The next day, Nick returned to the spot. The elderberry bushes were bent, snapped, and broken where the creature had torn a hole through them. Huge prints were in the mud.

Nick related the incident to his grandmother, who told him that the area where he had encountered the creature had been known for at least fifty years as Yahoo Holler (Hollow) because of the frequency of sightings of the hairy beasts. The creature was called Yahoo because the scream it made sounded like Yaaay-hooo. The Yahoos would come up on people's porches. The grandmother's teacher was afraid to send her own children to school because of the Yahoos in the woods.

Standing on porches and peering into windows seems to be a favorite Bigfoot activity, judging from other reports. In 2004, a woman living in Ohio County near the border between West Vir-ginia and Ohio, and about thirty miles south of Steubenville, Ohio, reported a scary encounter with a Bigfoot who paid a home visit one night.

The woman, I'll call her Ann, lived in a house that was way up a hollow and backed up against a steep hillside. She and her family had heard strange screams, howls, and moans issuing from the woods around them, as well as the sounds of breaking branches, and had smelled a foul odor like wet dog or sulfur. After a summer of frequent frightening noises, the family installed a motion-detection light on the porch.

On the night of December 12, Ann got up around 1 A.M. to go to the bathroom. As she returned to her bedroom, the motion detector went on—and stayed on. The light normally went off in a few seconds if it was tripped by a raccoon or cat scurrying past, so Ann knew something big had to be standing outside. She stepped into her children's bedroom. What she saw literally stopped her breath.

Standing on the porch, peering into the window, was a creature with massive, muscled legs covered with shaggy coal-black hair. It towered over her at about eight feet in height. A straw blind was partially pulled down over the window. Ann could see the lower half of the creature through the glass and see the outline of the upper torso through the blind.

Ann froze in terror. The creature continued staring into the window and then turned and left, heading into the woods. Ann was too frightened to see where it went. She awakened her children and took them into her bedroom. She lay awake in fear all night, worried that the creature would return.

In the morning, it took all her courage to venture outside. She found no distinct footprints, but did find some muddy slide marks on the hillside. The experience, she reported, gave her the shakes whenever she thought about it. Something was out there that could come back at any time. Ann had the impression that it was curious about what was inside the house. Would its curiosity ever get the better or it and impel it to break inside?

Sightings of large, hairy ape humanoids have been reported all over the planet. The creature is best known as Bigfoot, a term that has become nearly generic in referring to large hairy ape humanoids. The term "Bigfoot" originated in 1958 in the *Humboldt Times* newspaper in Eureka, California. The paper covered a story about huge footprints found in a logging camp in Bluff Creek in northern California. Ray L. Wallace, a native of Missouri, was working as a logger there and went on to become a Bigfoot researcher.

There are other names besides the Yahoo mentioned previously. In the Pacific Northwest, it is called Sasquatch, from the Salish word for "wild man" or "hairy man." In Florida and the southern United States, it is known as the Skunk Ape. In Australia, it is the Yowie and in New Zealand it is the Great Hairy Moehau. In the Himalayas, the creature is called a Yeti (also known as the Abominable Snowman) and in Russia the Alma, in Tibet the Kangmi, and in the Caucasus Mountains the Kaptar. To Nicaraguans, it is the monkey-man Xipe and Guatemalans call it El Sisemite.

Are all these creatures related? Some researchers think that Bigfoot is a remnant of a species known as *Giganto pithecus*, a giant ape up to ten feet tall that resided in China and Southeast Asia about 300,000 to 500,000 years ago and may have reached North America via a land bridge that once existed across the Bering Sea to Alaska. *Giganto pithecus* is believed to have become extinct.

Stories about such wild and hairy creatures appear in Native American lore long before the coming of the Europeans. One of the earliest European accounts comes from Spanish naturalist Jose Mariano Mozino as he accompanied Juan Francisco de la Bodega y Quadra on his exploration of the British Columbian coast in 1792. Mozino wrote about a monstrous "Matlox," covered in black animal hair with a human head, long sharp teeth, and huge arms that struck terror in the local inhabitants.

Some Native Americans, such as those in the West and Pacific Northwest, consider Bigfoot to be a real, physical creature, a "brother" who is a dweller of the forests. Others elsewhere, such as the Hopi, Sioux, and Iroquois, regard it as more of a supernatural entity whose appearances are deliberate for the purpose of bringing messages.

Whatever it is, Bigfoot graduated from myth and legend to mainstream pop culture in 1967, when two men, Roger Patterson and Bob Gimlin, produced a short film clip showing what they claimed was a Bigfoot they encountered in the Six Rivers National

Forest area in northern California, an area reputed to have many Bigfoot sightings. Patterson said he became interested in Bigfoot after reading a magazine article by Ivan T. Sanderson in 1959. He had plans to film a movie about a miner and an Indian tracker on the hunt for Bigfoot and reportedly hoped to capture footage of the real thing. Gimlin, who accompanied him, was skeptical about the existence of the creature. The two men were on horseback when they came upon Bigfoot. Patterson got off his horse and filmed the creature as it strode away from them, swinging its long arms and at one point turning its head to look back at them. The torso appeared to have breasts, leading to the conclusion that the creature was female. The clip, generally called the Patterson-Gimlin film, or simply the Patterson film, is fifty-three seconds long, and it created a sensation, propelling an ongoing interest in Bigfoot. Not everyone thinks the footage is genuine, however.

Bigfoot Traits

Bigfoot is usually described as being between six and eight feet tall, sometimes nine feet or more. It is proportioned like a human, but with a thicker neck, head, and body, and is covered in hair like an ape, either dark or reddish-brown, sometimes straight and sometimes shaggy. Its body also can be lanky or well-muscled, and it has long arms that extend below the knees. It walks easily upright, without having to use its knuckles, and can move at astonishing speeds through thick forest. Footprints measure up to twenty-four inches in length. It has bright eyes, often described as glowing, perhaps because of reflected headlight and flashlight shine at night.

In January 2007, a man who did not believe in Bigfoot came face to face with the creature he thought could not possibly exist. The encounter occurred around 11:30 P.M. as he was driving south on Route 55 near Seneca Rocks in Pendleton County, an area where others have had Bigfoot sightings. He suddenly spotted a figure running at a "swaggering lope." At first he thought it was a man, perhaps dressed in some sort of special forces gear, and then he realized that it was completely covered in hair that seemed to have clumps of material hanging from it. It was very tall, with wide shoulders and arms that hung to or below the knees. It trotted along like a man but with the movements of an ape. The witness passed it and turned his truck and U-Haul trailer around to get a better look. The creature was gone, but he could hear it crashing through the brush. It made weird laughing, squealing, and grunting sounds and made cracking noises like two giant pieces of wood being slammed together. After about five minutes, the commotion stopped. The next day the witness went back and saw large footprints.

Bigfoot often packs a monstrous stench, sometimes described as wet dog or a stinky human. One man described a horrible smell that spread through the woods on Spruce Flat Mountain in the Monongahela National Forest as "like a dirty, sweaty man who hadn't took a bath in a few years."

Bigfoot has several notable behaviors. One is throwing stones and large sticks at humans while remaining hidden, perhaps to scare them. The rock and stick throwing seems to be more of a warning than a deliberate attempt to injure, for the rocks usually miss people.

Another is making sharp knocking sounds on trees, like the crack of a baseball bat, and breaking and snapping tree limbs, small trunks, and dense foliage. The cracking noises, like the stone and rock throwing, may be intended to scare humans. Limbs and trunks of substantial thickness are snapped as though they were twigs, often at a height of about six to eight feet.

The creatures make a whooping sound, like woop-woop-woop-*whooo* or woooooop-woop-woop-woop, and also a rapid-fire gibberish, like someone speaking an unknown foreign language or talking backwards. In December 1997, a man was out hunting with his son early one morning in Nicholas County near the boundary of the Cranberry Wildlife Preserve when they heard "weird sounds" coming from a nearby gully. At first it sounded like a woman screaming, and then it turned into chatter, like a recording of a human speaking that was being played backwards.

In the summer of 1980 in the Huntington Spring Valley area of Cabell County, two men went to a favorite lake for a nighttime fishing trip. They had settled in for about half an hour when they heard what sounded like unseen people talking about forty yards away. They could not make out any words; it sounded like people talking backwards. While they were trying to make sense out of it, one witness said, "All of a sudden there was a hair-raising, blood-curdling *scream* from just up the hill behind us. I cannot possibly explain how frightening this sound was other than to say my whole body went limp with fear it felt like my legs were jelly." He looked over at his fishing buddy, whose face revealed he was just as terrified, and said, "What the hell was *that*?" Then men left "in an extreme hurry."

The sounds allegedly made by Bigfoot will spook animals. In July 2009, a resident of rural McDowell County was sitting on his porch late at night when bone-chilling screams issued from the woods, along with the sounds of something large crashing through the trees. There followed moaning howls and growls. The man's dogs were quite frightened and began a frenzied barking, joined by the dogs of his neighbors. The weird sounds went on for about four hours. The next day, the man learned that his neighbor's horses, which were out in a field that night, were badly spooked, and would not leave the barn the next morning, even for their food.

Stories of terrifying nights in remote areas raise questions about whether or not Bigfoot is hostile to humans and likely to be aggressive. Campers and hikers have felt threatened, and people who live in isolated areas have described hairy ape-men who assault their homes as though they are seeking to break in.

Others tell much different stories. In many encounters, Bigfoot seems merely curious about people, staring at them and then turning and walking away. Bigfoot contactees, who say they have had communication with the creatures, describe them as social, intelligent, and gentle—and perhaps more wary of us than we are of them. According to Kewaunee Lapseritis, a social scientist, the Bigfoot are willing to share information about themselves, human history, and the future of the planet—which puts a whole new spin on "monster" sightings.

Tracking Bigfoot

Many organizations collect and organize information on the thousands of Bigfoot sightings around the world. One of the largest is the Bigfoot Field Researchers Organization (BFRO), an Internet scientific community founded in 1995 by Matthew Moneymaker, a lawyer in California. Moneymaker launched BFRO while attending law school.

The BFRO was the first major website to collect Bigfoot reports, especially on a wide scale. The reports published have been investigated by experienced researchers to determine the credibility of the reports. For example, some accounts may be too vague, or some sightings may be determined to be known animals mistaken for Bigfoot.

At minimum, the witnesses must be willing to be interviewed. Investigations of reports may also involve field searches with experienced researchers, trackers, and wildlife experts, and lab analyses of any collected evidence, such as hair or stool samples. Reports that are published are graded A or B depending on their quality. There is a Class C for secondhand and thirdhand reports, but because of their unreliability, they are kept in the database but rarely listed publicly.

Since its inception, and as of this writing, the BFRO has published eighty-plus reports in West Virginia. These are probably but a fraction of actual sighting and encounters. Many people make no reports. Of the reports submitted to the BFRO, only about one in four has enough substantiating detail to warrant inclusion, according to Moneymaker. The reports are listed by county and include details from the witnesses and any follow-up comments from BFRO investigators. The information is used on Google Maps to identify target areas and thus illuminate patterns of appearances and behavior that will aid efforts to capture hard evidence— or even one of the creatures.

Moneymaker had his own personal Bigfoot encounter in eastern Ohio. At around 2 A.M., out in the woods, he suddenly saw an eight-foot-tall hairy creature. It growled at him, he said, letting Moneymaker know he was in the "wrong place." He had been searching for Bigfoot for years. In the woods of eastern Ohio, he claims, he finally came eye to eye with the elusive primate.

Bigfoot researchers often take to the wilds to look for evidence and to have, hopefully, their own sightings and encounters. Sometimes expeditions of researchers are mounted for intensive, coordinated investigations in hot spot areas. The searches for trace evidence are best done during daylight hours. Nights are devoted to vigils for sightings, encounters, and capturing sounds associated with Bigfoot. The creature seems to be mostly (but not exclusively) nocturnal in habits, and the greatest number of sightings occurs during the night.

Investigators play recorded sounds like the whoops, screams, howls, and chatter that are believed to have been made by real Bigfoot, to try to get an imitated response. They also make calls themselves. They examine the terrain for physical trace evidence, such as footprints, hair, and stool.

The BFRO has mounted Bigfoot expeditions in various states and in Canada. Expeditions in West Virginia in 2005, 2006, and 2008 have focused on the Greenbrier River Valley in Pocahontas County. The expeditions were led by BFRO researcher Stephen Willis, a native of Cowen, West Virginia, who now lives in Virginia. Willis had once spotted a Bigfoot in northern California.

In 2005, two possible Bigfoot were briefly spotted by Kathy Willis, Stephen's wife, during an afternoon. The lanky figures were walking in a leisurely manner along the river trail. At first she thought they were other members of the party and then realized that everyone was bundled up wearing thick and colorful raingear. Willis's sighting was the only visual encounter, but others heard sounds that included a howl, and splashes like rocks being thrown into the river, or something large walking in the river shallows. At one point a stick the thickness of a baseball bat came flying out of the trees, as though thrown.

In 2006, a group of thirteen investigators said three Bigfoot threw rocks at them while they hiked a trail along a tributary stream at night. One of the creatures became briefly visible when an investigator shined a headlamp into the darkness. The next day, they found partial footprints that indicated the creatures had been only about fifteen feet away from them.

In 2008, Willis led a group of twenty back to the Greenbrier River Valley for a four-day expedition. No visual encounters occurred, but the group heard the characteristic sharp wood knocks at night, and saw tracks, one eighteen inches in length and one thirteen inches, that may have been made by a Bigfoot.

Not surprisingly, counties in the Monongahela National Forest area—an ideal "haunt" for elusive creatures—have the highest concentration of sightings in West Virginia. The "Mon," as it is known, covers 919,000 acres, of which 94,991 acres are designated wilderness areas. Ten counties touch the Mon. The highest mountains in the state are here—Spruce Knob reigns at 4,863 feet—and they are covered with thick forests.

The BFRO has the most reports for counties that have territories within the Mon: Pendleton, Pocahontas, Tucker, Webster, Nicholas, Greenbrier, and Raleigh.

The Canyon Monster Wave

Paranormal phenomena sometimes come in waves in certain geographic areas, where sightings and encounters increase dramatically. Waves can last a few days to many years. They often start suddenly and stop suddenly, without apparent explanation. There are waves of UFO sightings (often called "flaps") and mysterious creature sightings. Mothman was part of a wave. There are Bigfoot waves as well.

West Virginia had its own Bigfoot wave when a creature dubbed the Canyon Monster was seen from about 1960 to 1975. The sightings were concentrated in mountainous Tucker County, located at the northern edge of the Mon. Part of the county touches the sharp tip of the end of the Maryland panhandle. Sightings occurred in other nearby counties that incorporate part of the Mon.

Many of the sightings were near the small town of Davis, located along the Blackwater River. In the summer of 1960, a group of young men went camping in the woods near Davis. One night, one of them was cutting firewood for their campfire when he felt a poke in the ribs and heard a noise. He thought it was one of his companions, but when he turned, he was confronted with a "horrible monster." His companions saw it, too. The young man told John Keel in a letter, "It had two huge eyes that shone like big balls of fire and we had no light at all. It stood every bit of eight feet tall and had shaggy long hair all over its body. It just stood and stared at us. Its eyes were very far apart."

The youths froze in shock. The creature turned and ambled off into the dark woods. The young men were spooked but stayed at their campsite. Nonetheless, they left earlier than planned in the morning. In the light of day, they saw huge footprints in the earth where the creature had been standing and which led into the woods. They were too frightened to follow them.

Near Parson, another town in Tucker County, multiple witnesses reported seeing the same or similar creature in the summer of 1960.

In October 1960, a similar "thing" confronted a man in an automobile near the tiny town of Edray, population thirty-five, in Pocahontas County. That creature was automatically labeled the "Braxton Monster" by the media, though descriptions bore no resemblance to the entity seen in 1952.

A huge creature with eyes that "shone like big balls of fire" ruined the electrical system of a car, according to witness and car owner W. C. "Doc" Priestley of Alum Creek in Kanawha County. In a letter to the *Beckley Post-Herald* that was published on January 4, 1961, Priestley said, "I have definite proof that the hairy monster is real." The article acknowledged that "apparently" Priestley was referring to the Braxton Monster, though Priestley never named it as such. But his description of the beast, and especially its huge, glowing eyes, bears a striking similarity to the Davis-area sighting a few months earlier.

Edray is located in the heart of the Monongahela National Forest, about three miles north of Marlinton and about thirty-five miles from the 1952 Braxton sightings.

Priestly said he and two companions were heading into the forest for turkey-hunting season. He was driving alone in his car and his two companions, Gene Williams Foresi and Mont Priestley, rode ahead in a camping bus. They traveled up Williams River for about an hour. Suddenly Priestley's car, which had been "purring like a kitten," started to sputter and misfire, and then it came to a stop.

"Then I saw it," Priestley said. "To my left beside the road stood this monster with long hair pointing straight up toward the sky. I was so scared I could not move. I don't know how long I sat there until the boys missed me and backed the bus back to where I was. It seemed the monster was very much afraid of the bus and dropped his hair and to my surprise as soon as he did this, my car started to run again."

The creature disappeared and Priestley's companions did not see it. He decided not to mention the beast. He resumed driving, but his car started to act up again. "I could see the sparks flying under the hood of my car as if it had a very bad short," he said. "And sure enough there beside the road stood the monster again."

Priestley fell behind the bus, and the other men backed it up to look for him again. The creature disappeared again, but Priestley's car was dead, the points "completely burned out." He still did not confide in his companions, fearing that if they knew a monster was in the woods, they would not return with him later in the year for deer-hunting season. By January 1961, Priestley evidently decided to speak up.

The creature's hair standing straight up sounds like a charge of static electricity. Was it reacting to the electricity generated by the car engine? Or was the creature generating its own energy field that interfered with the car?

A couple of months later, on December 31, 1960, the same or a similar creature was seen along the roadside in another location, but there was no hair standing on end. The sighting was terrifying enough, however, to prompt the formation of a gun-toting posse. Sightings were not limited to Tucker County. Charles Stover, twenty-five, a Clay County bakery truck driver, was driving alone near Hickory Flats between Webster and Braxton Counties at about 11 P.M. Suddenly he saw a six-foot humanoid monster, completely covered with hair, standing erect by the side of the road. Astonished, Stover stopped and backed up while the creature watched. Now frightened, Stover roared off. After he calmed down, he pulled into a roadside restaurant for a cup of coffee and related his experience to the people present. The alarmed men formed an impromptu posse, armed themselves with shotguns and rifles, and went off in search of the monster. They did not find it, but did discover upturned rocks at the spot where Stover had seen the creature. The monster had vanished into the depths of the woods—or perhaps into another dimension. "Weird cries" were heard in the area for weeks after that.

Throughout the fifteen-year wave, so many sightings of the creature were reported by campers, hikers, and horseback riders that locals started calling it the "Canyon Monster." Most descriptions said it was eight to nine feet tall, had a hair-covered body like an ape, had a hairless face, and walked on two legs. Were all the sightings of the same creature, or were there more than one with similar appearances? The answer is not known.

The Evidence for Bigfoot

Many, if not most, Bigfoot researchers support the forgotten species explanation for Bigfoot. But if Bigfoot is a real, physical creature, the hard evidence for its existence remains slim despite several decades of intense investigations. Researchers have taken plaster casts of numerous huge footprints that defy explanation and have collected hair and stool samples determined by laboratory analyses to be of unknown origin. While tantalizing and convincing, the evidence still falls short of scientific proof. Photographs and videos of big hairy-looking forms have been taken and likewise still fall short of proof; many of them are blurry or taken from too far a distance to be conclusive as to the creature.

Compromising the evidence collected by sincere researchers are the hoaxes perpetrated by people for a variety of reasons. Whenever a hoax is exposed, skeptics tend to throw the baby out with the bathwater by declaring that the hoaxes discredit *all* evidence. Sometimes, however, even the hoaxes themselves are questionable.

After Ray L. Wallace died at age eighty-four in 2002, his children made an announcement that the 1958 Bluff Creek, California, footprints were a big prank, done by Wallace with carved wooden feet. Michael Wallace, one of his sons, was quoted in the *New York Times* stating, "This wasn't a well-planned plot or anything. It's weird because it was just a joke, and then it took on such a life of its own that even now, we can't stop it."

Without Wallace alive to agree or disagree, the alleged hoax may never be truly resolved. Bigfoot researchers point to the large number of unexplained gigantic footprints discovered all over the world as evidence that the hoax story does not hold.

Perhaps the most brazen hoax occurred in 2008, when two men in Georgia announced they had a supposed Bigfoot carcass in a freezer. The story was expertly hyped by a third man and was carried by thousands of newspapers and media outlets all over the world. The corpse was soon exposed as a rubber dummy dressed in a Halloween gorilla costume, stuffed with animal parts that began to rot as the "carcass" was defrosted. The DNA evidence offered turned out to be opossum. The case became clouded by a lawsuit filed over funds allegedly paid for the body. The fake Bigfoot was put up for sale on ebay as a way to resolve the dispute, according to a spokesperson.

The Patterson film of 1967, showing the female Bigfoot striding away with swinging arms, has been studied by dozens of experts. In terms of scrutiny, it is cryptozoology's equivalent of the Zapruder film of the assassination of President John F. Kennedy.

Experts have examined every possible perspective to assess whether the creature was an animal or a human in a disguise and to gauge its height, weight, length of stride, motion, gait, and so forth. Anthropologists, primate experts, artists, costume designers, and anatomists have been among those weighing in with both pro and con opinions over the authenticity of the film.

The motives of Patterson have been subject to scrutiny as well. Was this a lucky find by a Bigfoot enthusiast, or was it a staged money shot for profit and fame? Critics have contended that Patterson was desperate for money. In 2004, author Greg Long published a book, *The Making of Bigfoot: The Inside Story*, in which he made a case for Patterson's "Bigfoot" being a man in an animal suit. The man was identified as Bob Hieronimus, a native of Yakima, Washington, who at the time was twenty-six years old. Not everyone in the field accepted Long's account. Patterson, who died in 1972, always insisted the footage was real. Gimlin, who has made occasional appearances at Bigfoot conferences, has denied participating in a hoax. The debate still rages on.

Paranormal Possibilities

Some researchers, myself included, favor the paranormal, interdimensional explanation: Bigfoot is real, but belongs to another dimension, and has forays into our world. This may explain the lack of substantial hard evidence. They seem to enjoy some of the food supply here, so perhaps they know how to find ways into certain places, via portals, where they can "come over" for a meal. Many witnesses sense a keen intelligence in the creatures, so deliberate forays to an exotic feeding ground might not be a far-fetched idea.

"I personally feel that there is a multidimensional aspect to most cryptids," Lon Strickler told me in an interview. "In July 2010 I posted a poll on the Phantoms and Monsters blog that posed the question, 'What is Bigfoot/Sasquatch?' To my surprise, 26 percent of the 574 participants answered that they believed this creature is an interdimensional or extraterrestrial being. Are we at a point where people are open-minded enough to accept that a hominid species may very well not be of our time or planet?"

Don Keating, the founder of the Eastern Ohio Bigfoot Investigation Center, is among researchers who favor a physical explanation but are open to an interdimensional one.

"My own personal belief is that we are dealing with a physical, flesh and blood animal," Keating told me in an interview. "But I'm open-minded to every possibility. The only evidence we have so far are footprints. We haven't found a body yet, and that is a sticking point. However, there may be so few of them that finding their remains is much more difficult than finding a dead deer along the highway."

The idea that Bigfoot lives in another dimension is not new. As mentioned earlier, many Native American beliefs hold that Bigfoot is a supernatural entity who lives in another realm. Their appearances are not accidental, but for the purpose of delivering messages to people, especially in bad times. The "Big Man" according to the Lakota is both spirit and real, able to glide easily through the forests and even shape-shift into animal forms. The Big Man looks out for humans and appears when people have strayed from their spiritual path and need to get reoriented with a spiritual cleansing.

According to the Hopi, the "big hairy man" is but one form that the Creator's messenger takes when it come to warn all humanity of the need to correct its evil ways. In the east, the Algonkian associate Bigfoot with the Ho chunk, formerly known as the Windigo, a huge spirit of a human turned into a supernatural cannibal, who eats human flesh in times of starvation. The Ho chunk stands more than six feet tall, has long, stringy hair, and smells like a rotting corpse. It runs faster than a human, is stronger than a grizzly bear, breathes fire, and howls like the wind. It has a heart of ice. White settlers regarded the Ho chunk as a banshee-like omen of death of a family member.

In either guise, as a helper to humanity or as a messenger of spiritual warning, death or doom, Bigfoot dovetails with similar experiences involving extraterrestrials.

Bigfoot, UFOs, ETs, and Beyond

A curious connection exists between Bigfoot sightings and UFO activity: The two sometimes happen in conjunction with each other, or both happen repeatedly in the same areas. Many of these connections are overlooked by researchers in both camps. For example, some years ago, I had a conversation with a Bigfoot researcher who spent quite a bit of time in the woods at night, with a great deal of sophisticated surveillance equipment, hoping to capture evidence of Bigfoot. I asked him if he ever saw any UFO activity and he replied that he often did, and he even captured some of it on his equipment—but it was of no interest to him. I have found similar disinterest in Bigfoot among ufologists.

Fortunately, there are growing numbers of researchers who are realizing that all strange phenomena and entity encounters are interconnected in some way, and a broader perspective is required. Even in the 1970s, a few pioneers in ufology, among them Stan Gordon, Loren Corenzen, and Peter Guttila, began noting and documenting the connection between Bigfoot and ET/UFO activity.

In his book *Silent Invasion: The Pennsylvania UFO-Bigfoot Casebook* (2010), Gordon documented a wave of Bigfoot and UFO activity from 1973 and 1974 around Uniontown and Greensburg, Pennsylvania, in Fayette County, a hot zone of paranormal activity that lies just across the state line thirty miles north of Morgantown, West Virginia. The activity in Fayette County, still a hot spot, spills into West Virginia.

A few years before the Fayette County flap, John A. Keel documented Bigfoot reports along with the mélange of high strangeness in the Mothman flap in Point Pleasant.

Cryptozoologist Loren Coleman notes there is now a considerable body of literature documenting the Bigfoot-ET/UFO connection. Author and investigator Nick Redfern, always willing to plunge into a controversial topic, notes that "the fact of the matter is that there is surely not a Bigfoot researcher out there who has not been exposed to (at the *very* least) a few creature cases that absolutely *reek* of high-strangeness, and that place the hairy man-beasts into definitively Fortean—rather than zoological or cryptozoological—realms."

Redfern continues, "Whether those same Bigfoot researchers are willing to admit they have come across such cases—or are willing to give such reports some degree of credence—is a very different matter, however!"

Bigfoot sightings, footprints, and other trace evidence have been collected in other areas where UFO activity has been documented. Joe Fex of Denver, Colorado, the founder and curator of the APE-X Research Archives, has collected reports of intelligent Bigfoot with connections to ETs. Kewaunee Lapseritis became a simultaneous Bigfoot and ET contactee in 1979. In his book *The Psychic Sasquatch and Their UFO Connection* (2005), Lapseritis describes Bigfoot as intelligent, psychic, and telepathic beings who work with extraterrestrials as guards and scouts. People who become Bigfoot contactees can have telepathic communication with them. One individual, R. Scott Nelson, has assembled a "Sasquatch phonetic alphabet."

Reports such as these tread too deeply into fringe territory for many cryptozoologists and Bigfoot researchers, but others are willing to let the jury sit out, arguing that we cannot make assumptions that Bigfoot is a remnant of an earthly prehistoric species.

The cross-connection of Bigfoot and UFO sightings strengthens the argument for portal areas, places where all manner of paranormal and unexplained phenomena may happen. Such areas are likely to include other mysterious creature sightings and ghost activity as well.

Mystery Dogs, Demon Dogs, and Werewolves

A voracious creature called the Blue Devil terrorized the vicinity of Webster Springs, Webster County, from 1939 to 1940 and was blamed for the killing of a hunting dog and for attacking livestock. The creature was described as dog-faced, bluish in color, about the size of a pony, and resembling a wolf or coyote. It screamed like a banshee or a panther. The creature prowled the Grassy Creek and Jumbo areas at night, but was seldom actually seen, sparking debates as to whether or not it actually existed.

In 1939, John Clevenger of Jumbo said the Blue Devil killed one of his most valuable hunting dogs while the dog was trailing it through the forest, according to a report in the *Charleston Daily Mail* on December 13 of that year. Ernest Cogar, also of Jumbo, said the Blue Devil had frightened his sheep and cattle, causing them to mill about restlessly at night. One of the cattle was attacked and wounded by an unknown animal, believed to be the Blue Devil.

Posses of hunters from Charleston, Buckhannon, and Webster Springs tried to track it down without success. Hunters from other states were attracted to the mystery. Two hunters from New York City brought their hunting dogs and picked up a scent around Jumbo late one night. The dogs took off but came slinking back after midnight and refused to follow the scent again.

So many reports circulated that residents considered petitioning the state conservation commission to either mount a hunt to slay the beast or conduct an investigation to prove it did not exist. Newspapers treated the subject with ridicule. The *Charleston Gazette* dismissed the Blue Devil as a giant mole, and the *Wheeling News-Register* expressed no interest at all in "strange animals."

Regardless of whether a supernatural Blue Devil was on the loose, it was a fact that something was killing sheep.

In December 1939, a man claimed to have killed the Blue Devil. Glen Fisher, of the Bill Fisher hollow, told the press that he shot a mystery animal one night earlier that jumped up in the air as the bullet struck it. He waited until morning to see what he had killed, but no carcass could be found. Fisher claimed that there had been no sightings of the Blue Devil since then.

Apparently the creature migrated elsewhere, because ranchers in the Elk River and Middle Mountain areas reported a marauder had attacked and killed sheep and reportedly even attacked men on several occasions. Residents put up a bounty reward of about two hundred dollars for the killing of the Blue Devil, an amount to be matched by the state conservation commission, and the Valley Head Rod and Gun Club put up another twenty-five dollars.

On December 5, 1940, a coal miner from Weaver claimed he was the one to finally kill the Blue Devil, and was entitled to the reward money. Elmer Corley said he was not positive about the identity of the beast, but he was confident it was the mystery animal. The carcass was examined by C. T. Whittacre, the district game protector, who said it looked like a coyote, but he was not certain of its identity.

Monster dogs and doglike creatures with occult powers and bizarre or hideous appearances are common in supernatural lore around the world. Like the Blue Devil, they sometimes embody the characteristics of multiple animals, but are mostly doglike in appearance. Some of them can run either on all fours or on their hind legs—and at amazing speeds.

The Webster Werewolf

If the Blue Devil really was killed, then what was the werewolflike creature encountered in Webster County years later? Were there more than one?

Two young cousins and their fathers joined other hunters at a deer camp on Cranberry Ridge late one November. The camp was well off the roads and deep into the mountainous terrain. The day was unusually warm, and a heavy rain set in by evening.

The father and uncle discovered they had forgotten to bring lard for cooking dinner, so the two cousins volunteered to drive an all-terrain vehicle (ATV) into Nicholas County to buy some, as well as some other items and groceries. They put on their rain gear and set off across Tunnel Ridge. As they approached the Gauley River, the rain eased and the cloud cover broke to reveal moonlight.

The youths got stuck in mud holes and had to stop to push the ATV out. At one point, they stopped to take off their rain gear and check on their gas tank. As they stood by their vehicle, one of the youths saw what appeared to be an enormous wolf standing on its hind legs behind them on the trail. It was visible only in silhouette. It had a long snout, long and pointed ears, was completely covered in hair or fur, and stood about six-and-a-half feet tall. "Werewolf!" flashed through the witness's mind.

He stood frozen and speechless and then managed to stammer, "Look!" His cousin turned and saw the creature staring at them. The two jumped on the ATV and tore off. They were so frightened they could not look behind them, lest they see the monster in hot pursuit. The driver was so scared he forgot to shift out of first gear and nearly ruined his ATV.

The youths made it to the uncle's house, where they spilled their story to his wife. They refused to drive back to camp alone, so they loaded the ATV into a pickup truck and asked the wife to drive them back.

The others at the camp were surprised to see the youths arrive in the truck with the ATV in the back. When the boys told their story, no one believed them—everything had been normal at camp.

The Red-Eyed Wolf-Bear

In the spring of 1980, a couple went out for a hike near Yawkey in Lincoln County. The young man intended to propose to his girlfriend atop the peak of a mountain that afforded a spectacular view. It was a proposal they would never forget, for they came upon a creature not known in this world.

Between 3 P.M. and 4 P.M., they were on a narrow and steep trail deep in the woods when they heard what sounded like a bear in the thicket, coming toward them up the trail. Bears are common in the area, and the couple instinctively froze in silence. Because of the heavy brush, the couple could see nothing. The creature seemed not to notice them as it moved through the brush.

Then the creature stepped out onto the trail about twenty to thirty feet in front of them. What the couple saw was no bear, but some monstrous hybrid creature. It was furry and black, much larger than a bear, and had a long bushy tail and pointed snout like those of a wolf. It stank with a terrible odor. As the creature walked along on all four legs, the couple's hair stood on end. The man quietly maneuvered his girlfriend behind him.

The creature stopped and rose up on its hind legs, towering about seven feet in height. It stared at them with beady eyes that shone neon red. For a tense moment, the couple feared attack. Then the creature abruptly walked off the trail to the right on its hind legs and disappeared into the thicket. As it left, they noticed that its front legs, or "arms," were shorter than its hind legs.

When they returned home, the young man told his father what they had seen. His father, who grew up in West Virginia in the 1930s and '40s, said he had heard of this creature when he was a boy himself. It would come and prowl around the house at night and kill livestock. The family dogs were terrified of it and would crawl deep beneath the house. Everyone in the family could see this monster walking around the house, the top of its back visible in the windows. Even the ground shook as it walked. The house filled with a stench. No one would venture outside. In the morning, they would find a horse, cow, or other farm animal slaughtered.

The identity of the creature has never been determined, but it, or others like it, has been lurking in the Lincoln County woods for a very long time.

Black Dogs

Spectral or mystery black dogs roam lonely places all over the world. They jump out in the road in front of travelers, only to vanish an instant later. They are seen running at great speeds along empty beaches, marshes, fields, and forests, especially at night. They prowl through graveyards. Sometimes they have glowing red eyes, or their eyes are fiery green or yellow. Some of them are headless. They often are larger than the biggest known dogs, even as big as a calf.

Mystery black dogs go by many names, such as demon dogs, devil dogs, hell hounds, and yell hounds. In some places, they are known by proper names. The South Mountain region of Maryland has its Snarly Yow. In the Ozark Mountains, they are called Boogers. Devon, England, has the Whisht ("spooky") hounds, headless monsters that run the moors with their master, the pagan god Odin. Elsewhere in England, people talk about Black Shuck (Shuck is an alternate name for the Devil). This creature is headless, but has red eyes floating where a dog's eyes should be set. It is huge, and it wears a collar of chains that rattle as it runs. Black Shuck is also called Galleytrot, the Hateful Thing, the Shug Monkey, Hellbeast, Padfoot, and the Churchyard Beast. The first recorded Black Shuck sighting dates to 1577 in Bungay, Suffolk. In Scottish and Irish legend, the calf-sized dog is Cu Sìth, or "fairy dog," which has a dark-green coat, fiery eyes, and a curly and sometimes braided tail.

Are mystery black dogs ghosts, phantoms, or spirits, or are they physical creatures? Some are said to be phantoms, such as the ghostly dogs that guard the graves of persons who die unlucky deaths or phantom dogs that haunt the roads where people have died in vehicle accidents.

Many witnesses attest to their realistic, solid appearance, however, as well as their ability to disappear in a flash. For example, a person driving down a lonely country road at night rounds a bend and comes upon a black dog in the middle of the road. Or, a black dog suddenly lunges out from the darkness straight into the path of their oncoming car. The witness slams on the brakes, knowing that impact is certain—but the car goes right through the animal, which disappears. In some cases, there is the sound and feel of impact, but when the person is able to stop, get out, and look around, the car in not damaged, and there is no injured or killed animal anywhere to be seen.

All mystery animals share similar descriptions of "real but not real." At first sight the creatures seem real, and then witnesses realize there is something "unreal" or supernatural about them. They see the creatures one moment and not the next. There may indeed be ghostly dogs. But the monstrous black dog with an unworldly appearance may be a creature from another realm.

Black dogs are widely considered to be bad omens, foretelling death and disaster, much like the appearance of the banshee. It is considered unlucky in many parts of the world to see a spectral black dog. The bad omen connection appears again and again with mystery creatures of all kinds, including Bigfoot and Mothman.

West Virginia has its share of spectral hounds. Some seem to be ghosts. For example, in Harper's Ferry in Jefferson County, the ghost of John Brown is seen in town walking the ghost of his black dog. In Jackson County, in the Tug Fork area near Mill Creek, a huge, headless black dog has been seen for many years.

Other sightings lean more toward mysterious creature. In Parkersburg, in Wood County, numerous sightings have been reported of a huge black dog in the haunted Riverview Cemetery—though it is a puzzle how the animal is able to enter the locked and fenced grounds at night. The dog is much too large to have squeezed under the chain-link fence. People see the dog wandering about the tombstones. Every now and then it stops to dig and scratch at the earth. Sometimes it is followed by three black crows that sit on the headstones and watch as it digs. The dog disappears in trees near a tombstone called the Weeping Woman. The Weeping Woman is a statue of a mournful woman draped across the back and top of a tombstone, as though she has flung herself against it to grieve the dead below. According to lore, on certain nights the "Lady" stands up and wanders through the cemetery, wringing her hands and crying for all the souls lost in the Civil War. Is the black dog one of her guardians?

Paranormal researcher Susan Sheppard, who lives in Parkersburg, received an account from a woman whose visit from a black dog coincided with the death of a friend of her mother. The witness, a nurse, tended to the woman, who was hospitalized with a catastrophic stroke. She was not expected to survive the day, but she was still alive when it was time for the nurse to end her shift.

She left the hospital and walked out to the parking lot to her car. Suddenly a big black dog appeared seemingly out of nowhere—it did not come up from a distance, but was suddenly just "there." It fell in by her side. When she looked down at it, she was shocked to see the dog's face transform into the face of her stroke patient. Then it walked in front of her car and vanished.

The nurse was so shocked that she got down on her hands and knees and looked between cars for the dog, but it was nowhere to be found. A friend in the parking lot saw her and called out to her, asking what she was doing. The friend said she saw no black dog anywhere.

The nurse had an ominous feeling about her patient and looked at her watch. It was 4:10 P.M. Later she learned that the stroke patient had died at exactly the same time.

The "Incubus" of Calhoun County

A black dog described as an "incubus" reportedly attacked people who slept in a haunted bedroom in a house in the vicinity of Grantsville, Calhoun County, according to reports from the late nineteenth century. Whether the stories were hoax journalism cannot be determined, but the elements of the stories fit other such accounts. The black dog incubus is wrapped up in a ghost story as well.

The house in question belonged to Collins Betts, a farmer who lived in a rambling one-story house close to the Little Kanawha River, three miles south of Grantsville. For a time the home was used as the county courthouse before being moved to Brookville. According to accounts, the Betts house had a reputation at the time for being haunted. It was a frequent stopping place for travelers.

On September 30, 1884, the *Cincinnati Enquirer* ran an article about the "Cale Betts ghost," as it was known, and that it could not be "laid," or exorcized. The article said that numerous upright citizens had attested to the ghostly manifestations, which had been published in newspapers all over the country. Hundreds of letters had poured into the Betts homes with inquiries.

Betts tore down the original house and rebuilt his home on a different spot on his farmland. He hoped it would be the end of the ghost, but the ghost seemed to get riled up instead, and began pestering neighbors. It roamed for miles far and wide, frightening and distressing people, and eventually took up residence on a road, where it assaulted and terrified travelers. The article ended by saying that no one knew how to get rid of the thing.

That story resembles other stories of resistant ghosts, such as the Bell Witch spirit of Adams, Tennessee. By 1925, the story acquired a new phenomenon: A black demon dog. It was called an "incubus," although that term actually refers to a male demon that assaults women in their sleep. The black demon dog assaulted everyone.

On December 27, 1925, the *Charleston Daily Mail* updated the Cale Betts story. The article referred to the *Enquirer* story and then purported to reprint an article dated 1886. According to the article, the Betts house might have been haunted by a peddler who mysteriously disappeared and may have been murdered for the $1,000 he carried. A bedroom was haunted, and people who slept there were attacked by the demon dog. The "ghost" was believed to take other forms besides the black dog, including human, and to roam about outside the property. Once it appeared as a headless human to an overnight guest.

One night a Methodist minister named Rev. Wayne Kennedy spent the night and voluntarily slept in the haunted chamber. Sometime between midnight and 1 A.M., he awakened as a heavy weight came down on his chest, and he started to feel suffocated. He saw a huge black dog sitting on his chest. It took all of his strength to throw the "incubus" off. He departed in the morning, telling Betts he would not come back.

On another occasion, John Betts, the cousin of Collins, visited from Colorado and slept in the haunted room. He, too, was attacked at night. He was found lying in bed helpless, unable to move. He said he had been unable to throw the thing off, and the attack had lasted all night until dawn. He never fully recovered.

A man named Henry Elliott suffered a similar fate. He was turned into an invalid after being attacked by a huge black animal that nearly smothered him to death. Another visitor, Henry Newman, had an invisible animallike presence claw at his bedclothes.

The parade of victims went on. Young women saw "horrible phantoms." Terrified guests left in the middle of the night, galloping off on their horses. "Peculiar" shapes were seen. Whispery voices and odd sounds of heavy objects falling were heard. The mystery behind the manifestations remained unsolved.

It is puzzling that the black demon dog is not mentioned in the 1884 account, so perhaps the 1925 article was an embellishment for the purpose of Christmastime ghost storytelling, a custom in the past.

Even so, the characteristics described—a heavy black entity sitting on a person's chest with suffocating force—is a very real phenomenon documented for centuries. It has been called the

"Old Hag," a reference to the belief that a witch or demon attacked people at night and tried to kill them by pressing on the chest and suffocating them. Fact or fiction, the black dog in this account could be either phantom or unknown creature.

The "ghost" that takes many shapes also has been well documented. It cannot be said for certain that it is actually a ghost—the spirit of a dead person or animal—or is actually a creature or entity with the ability to shape-shift. Perhaps such creatures roam an area and become upset when people move in and build houses and other structures.

A Doglike Killer

A huge, doglike marauder roams the Sandy Huff Hollow Road near Iager in McDowell County. Hunters and recreational riders on all-terrain vehicles have seen it, and some hunters say they have been stalked by it. The creature runs on all fours but sometimes stands up on two hind legs and runs off into the woods. Missing chickens, cats, and pet dogs are believed to be the victims of this beast. A woman in a mobile home once reported that the thing appeared outside her home, and when it noticed her looking at it, peered into her windows. She raced about turning off all her lights, but the creature spent the entire night terrorizing her by banging and scratching on the home.

A Doglike Beast

In 2008, a large doglike creature was sighted at Hill Top Hill in Princeton in Mercer County. The witness reported the following:

Early in 2008, I was standing outside on my aunt's front porch holding a puppy that the neighbor's dog had just had. Suddenly I heard the sound of something big coming through thick brush. All of a sudden running down the edge of the hill, about 100 feet from where I was . . . I saw a weird creature. It looked like a huge dog. It was about as long as a horse, but was gray. It had doglike features, but a strange-shaped nose. It wasn't very aggressive. After I got over the initial shock, I made a loud noise at it. It didn't run away immediately, but after a few minutes this large creature ran off into the thick woods on the side of the hill and is probably still here somewhere.

A Strange Thing in Greenbrier County

In January 1998, three brothers went out rabbit hunting with a group of friends in Greenbrier County. Most of the day passed without sight of rabbits, and the hunting dogs seemed strangely uneasy. The dogs picked up a scent and ran up a hill. Then one dog peeled off to the side, barking frantically. The other dogs followed him. The hunters ran up the hill to see what was causing the commotion. When they reached the top, they saw a large, unknown creature running in a field. It was bigger than a dog, but not a bear. It ran at an amazing speed, looking back every few moments and baring its teeth. The creature vanished into the woods. Spooked and worried that the "thing" might attack the dogs, the hunters rounded up the animals and went home.

Strange Felines

Evil, malicious, and slantwise—those are the meanings behind the name Wampus Cat, the best-known mystery cat of the Appalachians and beyond. "Wampus" comes from the terms "catawampus" or "cattywampus," old terms used to refer to things that just aren't right. If you meet up with a Wampus Cat, bad luck and misfortune will strike. At the very least, you will go mad. The Wampus Cat is said to attack, maul, and kill farm animals, especially chickens, and to even attack humans.

The cat is described variously as a weird cross between a woman and a mountain lion; a cross between an oversized mountain lion, panther, or cougar and a gray wolf; a shape-shifted witch; or a hideous animal with a man's head and the soul of a demon. In some descriptions it has six legs, four for running as fast as lightning and two for strength in fighting. It is easily provoked and can tear anything to shreds.

Wampus Cat folklore and sightings concentrate in West Virginia, Virginia, Pennsylvania, the Carolinas, Georgia, Alabama, Kentucky, and Tennessee. The Flatwoods area in Braxton County, the center of the famous Braxton County Monster events in 1952, is home to generations of sightings of the Wampus Cat. The creature was even described as flying off into the air. In early accounts, the cat was considered to be a manifestation of the "Evil One," or the Devil.

White settlers who arrived in the Appalachians told of encounters with the Wampus Cat, a hideous being with hypnotic, glowing eyes that could walk erect on its hind legs. It had huge fangs and made terrible, unearthly screams. It preyed on domestic animals, children, and adults who were out at night hunting, fishing, or traveling through the woods.

Prior to colonization, the creature reigned in Native American lore, especially Cherokee, who called it the *Ewah*. According to one version of the story, a Cherokee woman did not trust her husband and decided to spy on him while he was out hunting with a group of men. She donned a coat or cloak made of a mountain lion skin and hid in the forest, eavesdropping. She was discovered and was forced to wear the coat forever, becoming half woman and half mountain lion. After she died, she became a ghostly Wampus Cat.

In another version of this tale, the woman spies on the men not because she is suspicious of her husband, but because she wants to learn the secret rites and magic taught to the men, knowledge that was forbidden to the women. When she was discovered, she was punished by the tribe's medicine man to take her monstrous form.

The story has still other versions. In another, different tale, the Wampus Cat was a creature that terrorized the Cherokee. A brave decided to kill it, but when he saw it, he went insane. His wife put on a mask and went out looking for the cat. She came up quietly behind it and screamed. The cat turned and when it saw her frightful mask, it fled and was never seen again. The woman's spirit, still wearing the mask, is still seen in the forests as the Wampus Cat.

One story told by white settlers combines the Native American beast with Christianized elements for dealing with demonic, evil beings, specifically the Word of God as the ultimate weapon. The story goes that a man went out hunting one night with his dogs and got the fright of his life. Suddenly they whimpered and took off from the path, and at the same time, a horrible stench filled the air. A terrible howl behind him caused the man to drop his rifle. He turned and saw an enormous Wampus Cat, standing on its hind legs, baring fangs that dripped saliva. It had huge, glowing eyes.

Screaming, the man dashed through the woods, pursued by the beast. He found the home of a friend and burst through the front door just as the Wampus Cat was about to seize him. The cat started slamming itself against the door. The friend immediately got out his Bible and started reading from the Psalms. The cat howled and retreated into the woods.

The man returned home at daybreak. He was glad to find his dogs there, hiding in the barn. He never again went out hunting at night.

In yet another version, told by white settlers who brought superstitions about demons and witchcraft with them to America, the Wampus Cat originated with a witch who lived alone. At night, she would turn herself into a large, golden-eyed, tuft-eared cat and went out to steal farm animals. She shape-shifted back into her female form in the day. Once, she was caught changing from cat to woman and remained half and half forever. Her face and part of her breast was woman and the rest of her was a monster cat. She fled into the woods and disappeared.

One version that circulated throughout West Virginia, combining the elements of Native American monster cat, witchcraft, and Bible remedies, concerned a man named Jinx Johnston. Jinx was a big brute who did not scare easily, except when he encountered the horrible Wampus Cat.

The cat was an old woman who lived alone in the West Virginian hills. Everyone knew she was a witch and suspected her of hexing and stealing farm animals. She would disguise herself as a cat, go to a neighbor's farm, and wait for someone to open the door. She hid in the house, and when everyone had gone to bed and fallen asleep, she would cast a spell to keep them asleep. She then slipped out—sometimes by going through the walls—to steal cattle and other farm animals. She also took things from the family that enabled her to cast more spells, such as personal objects, locks of hair, and so forth.

She never got caught. Finally, the locals could stand no more and came up with a plan to catch her. They hid in the barn, and when she tried to shape-shift back into human form, they pounced on her. Caught in mid-change, she was doomed forever to remain half cat and half woman. She wrestled free and fled into the night, roaming the land as the Wampus Cat, stalking farm animals and even children. She could be seen on hard windy nights when the moon was high, walking through the forests on her hind legs.

Jinx, who was fond of raccoon hunting at night, often heard the howls of the Wampus Cat. One night his dogs raced far ahead of him. He called for them to come back, but they did not return. Then he tripped on the path, and his rifle went flying out of his hands. Suddenly a horrible smell assaulted him, a stink like a skunk and a wet dog. Then he came face to face with the Wampus Cat. It had huge glowing eyes and fangs that dripped saliva. When it howled, he nearly jumped straight out of his own skin.

Jinx looked in desperation for his rifle, but could not see it in the dark. He made a break for home, running as fast as he could, the monster so close behind him that he could feel its hot breath on his neck. Jinx made it to safety and slammed and bolted the door behind him. Then he grabbed his Bible and read aloud. In response, the cat screamed and howled all night long. At dawn, it left. Jinx was so terrified that he never went coon hunting at night again.

Folklore often mutates over time; a more modern origin story of the cat dates to the mid-twentieth century. It is said that during World War II, the U.S. government conducted a secret program to crossbreed mountain lions and gray wolves in order to create a tough, formidable messenger. Some of the hybrids escaped and became Wampus Cats.

A host of other mysterious felines prowl the woods of the Mountain State. Some seem to be misplaced animals known to Earth, such as African lions and black panthers.

An Out-of-Place Lion

In the fall of 2007, several reports of an African lion roaming around Greenbrier County prompted officials to try to videotape and then capture the animal, but it disappeared without a trace. Was it really an African lion, or was it a mysterious creature that resembled one?

The hunt began after a seventy-two-year-old bow hunter, Jim Shortridge, had lengthy sightings of what appeared to be an adult male African lion with a mane. Shortridge was out hunting on his forty-acre ranch at Big Roaring Creek at the foot of Cold Knob. One morning at about 5:30, he was in his hunting shanty transferring his gear from his truck when he heard a large animal growling outside. Looking out, he saw the lion, pacing around the shanty. There was no way he could make a run for his truck, where he had left his bow, his only weapon.

Shortridge yelled at the animal and thought it ran off into the woods. He ventured outside and was able to retrieve his bow, but the animal came back and forced him back inside. For forty minutes, the lion paced around the building, huffing and growling. Shortridge, an expert hunter, gauged its weight at 250 to 300 pounds. He could not tell if it had a full mane.

The animal finally left without incident.

Shortridge notified the Division of Natural Resources, which said it had no jurisdiction over exotic animals. The Tiger Mountain Refuge in Rainelle, a nonprofit organization that rescues exotic animals, said they were not missing any large cats, including their own six-hundred-pound African lion. Owner John Forga said if another lion was loose, he would like to capture it and add it to the sanctuary.

West Virginia has no laws prohibiting the keeping of exotic animals as pets, and experts opined that the lion seen by Shortridge had been privately owned and either escaped from or was released by someone who wished to remain anonymous. If it was a pet, Forga said, it probably had been declawed and defanged and would likely not survive the winter.

After at least one other report of a lion in the same vicinity, officials took action. The state Department of Environmental Protection and Greenbrier County Animal Control set up game and motion-sensitive cameras and left twenty pounds of raw chicken as bait. They sprayed cologne on a nearby tree. The cologne was intended to attract the animal, which they hoped would claw the tree and leave evidence. If the lion showed up, their next plan was to set up a bear trap to capture it.

The meat was eaten, but no lion clawed the tree or was caught on camera. Officials said anything could have eaten the bait.

Meanwhile, the publicity generated by the lion hunt prompted a Charleston businessman, Angus Peyton, to offer a $3,000 reward for the safe capture of the creature. Peyton feared that someone would try to shoot and kill the lion, and he wanted to ensure that it would be delivered to the refuge.

The lion, or whatever it was, declined the bait and vanished. No carcass was ever found.

Black Panthers That Cannot Be

The experts say there is no such thing, yet black panthers are seen not only in West Virginia, but all over America. They are huge and ferocious, measuring about six feet in length and weighing about 250 pounds. Black panthers are not indigenous to North America but live in Africa, South America, and Asia. If the huge black cats seen in the wilds are not black panthers, then what are they? No one has a good answer.

There are two species of big cats in the Western Hemisphere: mountain lions and jaguars. Mountain lions (also called cougars in the West, pumas in the East, and panthers in the South) are the largest indigenous cat in North America. They are golden or tawny in color, and according to experts, do not have black offspring. Most live in the western United States, having lost their habitats in the East. Jaguars are the third-largest cat in the world, bigger than the mountain lion. They once lived in the western

United States but are thought to have been wiped out by the turn of the twentieth century. They sometimes have black offspring, but are thought not to venture farther north than the lower South.

Leopards, not indigenous to North America, can be black, but they do retain markings of their spots. Leopards seen in the wild probably would be escapees from captivity, experts say.

Mountain lions have been considered extinct in the East since the early 1900s, but sightings of them are frequent in modern times. West Virginian folk tales tell of mountain lions perching in trees to wait for prey to pass below, and screaming like "a woman dying." Hundreds of sightings of mountain lions have been reported in West Virginia since 1975.

The black panther is a cat literally of another color, since it is not supposed to exist at all in North America. Approximately ten to fifteen percent of all wild big cat sightings in the East involve "black panthers," and the majority of those sightings occur in Pennsylvania, Maryland, and West Virginia, according to the Eastern Puma Research Network.

So how should these alleged big black cats be classified? As a real but rare species, or as unknown cryptids? The state's Department of Natural Resources considers sightings of black panthers and mountain lions to be mistaken identities (domestic and feral cats, bobcats, fishers, wild dogs, or coyotes) or escaped exotic pets or zoo creatures. Most sightings occur at night, when viewing conditions are not optimum, and light-colored cats might seem to be black. The animal's screams are sometimes explained away as hoot owls. Indignant witnesses, many of whom are farmers and sportsmen, insist they know what they saw and heard.

Most of the black panther sightings in West Virginia are reported in the north central or eastern panhandle part of the state, including areas near the towns of Moorefield, Parsons, Davis, Thomas, Petersburg, Rowlesburg, and Grafton, as well as Bunners Ridge near Fairmont and Hundred in Wetzel County. Sightings are not limited to woods and remote areas. Black panthers have been spotted in suburban areas around cities such as the Kingwood Pike neighborhood of the busy university city of Morgantown.

In January 2005, a West Virginia farmer named Jason Bowers captured what appears to be a large black panther on video in southwestern Pendleton County. He, his wife, and a friend witnessed the cat prowling around on his property one clear morning.

The footage was shown on the History Channel's *Monster Quest* in December 2007. The animal was judged by experts who analyzed the film to be 24.92 inches from nose to rump, bigger than the average domestic cat, possibly a young but out of place jaguar or an escaped young leopard.

The show concluded that no evidence supports the existence of black panthers, and that large black cats, if they are not escapees from zoos or private collections, might be black leopards or jaguars making their way northward from Mexico to reestablish themselves in the United States. However, experts said no evidence exists of a breeding population of such cats, especially so far north as West Virginia.

One expert opined that seeing large black cats is all in the heads of the witnesses, stemming from age-old religious fears about black cats being the Devil or a demon. The subconscious fear supposedly causes witnesses to think they see a black cat (the Devil) when in fact it really is another color.

Despite the official stance, witnesses of so-called black panthers stand firm, suggesting that the officials know the real truth, but do not want to admit it and cause panic.

The Winged Cat of Pinesville

Winged cats are not unusual in the literature of mystery creatures, but sometimes they have ordinary explanations. The case of Thomas, the "winged cat" of Pinesville, Wyoming County, illustrates how much people want to believe in supernatural critters, despite the evidence.

Thomas was found in 1959 by a fifteen-year-old boy, Doug Shelton, who was out hunting with his dog one day in the woods.

The dog treed a creature, and Shelton was about to shoot it when he saw that it was a cat. He shimmied up the tree and captured it.

Thomas was no ordinary-looking cat. Two protuberances that looked like wings sprouted from its back. Irritated, the cat raised them like a bird raises its wings. Shelton took the cat home and named it Thomas. Word spread through the hills of his mysterious winged feline.

Fern Miniacs, a reporter for the *Post-Herald* in Beckley, made a trip to see the cat first-hand. She discovered that Thomas was a female (the name stuck, anyway) and was large for a cat, about thirty inches long. She had exceptionally large feet, long hair like a Persian cat, a long tail like a squirrel's, and two stubby but perfectly formed "wings." The wings appeared to be boneless but had gristle.

Experts soon examined Thomas. One thought the wings to be matted hair. A veterinarian from Baltimore, Maryland, had no explanation.

The cat made such a news splash that Shelton and Thomas were invited to appear on NBC's *Today Show*. Shelton told the audience that he had been offered four hundred dollars for Thomas, but he was not going to sell.

However, he and his family did charge money to see the cat. The curious paid a dime for viewing Thomas, and reporters were charged modest fees for snapping photos. Lines formed around the Shelton home. According to Doug, at least one thousand people came, which would have netted him about one hundred dollars—a nice profit in 1959.

The bubble burst when a neighbor announced that Thomas was really her cat, named Mitzi, who had disappeared from home about the time that Shelton found the cat. The Sheltons refused to surrender Thomas, so the neighbor, Mrs. Charles Hicks, sued.

The case went to trial on October 5, 1959. Shelton came with the cat—and a box bearing the "wings," which were nothing but large balls of hair. Shelton said the cat had spontaneously shed them. Mrs. Hicks said the cat was not her Mitzi. She was awarded one dollar for her trouble, and Shelton kept the cat.

With her wings gone, Thomas's fame faded as abruptly as it had blossomed. In 1966, John Keel passed through Pinesville and attempted to track down the Sheltons, Mrs. Hicks, and the cat, but to no avail.

White Things and Sheepsquatch

hite mystery creatures are well known to the mountain folk of West Virginia. Like black mystery dogs, they roam isolated, wooded areas. They appear in various shapes. In 2009, I met author Kurt McCoy, who acquainted me with a particularly fearsome white creature called the White Thing. Intrigued, I found more accounts of White Things in the folklore literature and in reports to such sites as wvtrueghoststories.com and phantomsand monsters.com.

McCoy, a native of Moundsville, West Virginia, and a current resident of Morgantown, became so fascinated by White Things that he collected and published eyewitness accounts. He found White Thing accounts in other states, but none matched the frequency of reports in West Virginia.

Even McCoy's own father had an encounter with a White Thing. When his father was a young boy, he spotted an odd creature on the fringe of the woods near his house. It looked like a cross between an impossibly large dog and a lion, and it was stark white with long shaggy hair.

White Things are described also as resembling wolves, bears, cows, and even huge badgers. They are covered with long, shaggy, snow-white or dirty-white hair, and they often have immense jaws and fangs. They move at lightning speed, sometimes on two legs rather than four. Sometimes they seem to have "too many legs." Their chilling screams sound like a woman being raped or murdered.

Whatever they are, they are bloodthirsty and attack without provocation. The attacks are so real that people actually "feel" the beast's fangs tearing into their flesh. But when the attack is over, they are shocked to find not a mark on their body. However, the beasts rip up animals in the fashion of a werewolf, tearing out their throats and mutilating their bodies—and leave the corpses bloodless and without a trace of blood around.

Most chilling of all, there is little defense against a White Thing. Bullets do not faze it. Curiously, White Things have an aversion to graveyards, much like a vampire has an aversion to garlic.

Many of the early stories about White Things date to the early twentieth century in an area known as Morgan's Ridge, near Morgantown. On a late night in July 1929, a Croatian immigrant named Frank Kozul was walking home alone from his shift at a coal mine. He decided to take a shortcut through the woods on Morgan's Ridge. It was a decision he would regret.

Kozul suddenly found himself confronted by a savage "thing." It was about two feet high at the shoulder and was built like a large dog with oversized jaws and a bushy tail. It was completely covered in white shaggy hair.

The creature stared at him for a few moments and then sprang, snapping its huge jaws and snarling. Kozul swang at it with his empty lunch pail, but the pail went right through the creature as though it were made of thin air. Kozul ran. The creature paced him, slamming against him. It had foul breath. But if Kozul tried to hit it or push it away, he connected with nothing solid.

Kozul stumbled and fell near a graveyard, and the White Thing vanished. When he got up, Kozul was surprised to see that he did not have a scratch, bite mark, or any kind of wound on him—yet he had definitely felt contact with the beast.

In another, more recent account from the late 1970s or early 1980s, a group of men went deer hunting out of season. Suddenly they heard an ungodly scream like a woman in agony. Before they could react, a White Thing tore out of the brush and leaped upon one of the hunters, knocking him to the ground. Man and beast rolled down a hill, both screaming. When his comrades found him, the hunter was lying on his back punching at air. He screamed that the beast had ripped out his guts. But not a mark was found on him. Shaken, he could not believe that he was not wounded, for he had felt the beast's teeth sink into his flesh. He had felt his entrails snapped out of his body. The hunters tried to convince themselves that the beast was a feral dog. The victim had nightmares for years.

Humans may come to no real physical harm from a White Thing attack, but animals are not so lucky. Ruth Ann Musick, a West Virginian folklorist, collected folktales in which White Things savagely mutilated and killed farm animals, such as horses and sheep.

Like all mysterious creatures, there are variations in descriptions of White Things and even labels. Some of the white mystery beings are called "White Devils," for they have red eyes and long, sharp claws, and are able to walk and run upright.

Some of the beasts have a connection to cemeteries, not an aversion, and thus are death-omen creatures. In another of Musick's stories, probably from the turn of the twentieth century, a husband and wife had to pass by a cemetery whenever they went to and from church in their horse and buggy. One winter night as they went by the cemetery, a White Thing that looked like a huge dog appeared and spooked the horses. A few weeks later, the same thing happened. The couple heard of similar experiences of others passing by the cemetery, and the wife became so frightened that she cowered down in the buggy whenever they passed it. After several years of these periodic and frightening episodes, the wife died and was buried in the very cemetery. The White Thing stopped appearing, which made some folks think that it had been waiting just for her.

Mystery creatures aren't always out for the attack—sometimes they are amusing themselves when people stumble upon them. In fairy lore, the fairies like to dance and jig at night, but woe be to the person who sees them—they will be struck blind.

McCoy relates a curious story about a young man from Kingwood. After driving his date home one night, the man got lost on the dark country roads. He stopped his car and then heard a commotion farther down the road, past a bend. He got out and walked toward it, expecting to find people, perhaps a local resident who could help him.

What he saw when he rounded the bend astonished him. There in the middle of the road was a weird creature. It was a bit shorter than he and was covered with long white shaggy hair like a sheepdog's. It had hands with fingers. It was hooting and hollering, jumping up high in the air, spinning around, and then landing with a grunt on its rear end. It dragged its rear on the ground like a dog wiping its butt, and then leaped up into the air again, hooting, hollering, and spinning.

The young man made a noise. The creature cried out like a surprised man, and then raced into the brush crying like a baby. Within moments it charged out at the young man, screeching like an owl, its hair standing straight on end. The young man dashed back to his car and frantically got inside. The creature, still shrieking, picked up handfuls of rocks and pelted the car. The young man leaned on the horn, startling the creature. It shouted and ran back into the woods on all fours.

Whatever White Things are, they do not seem to be flesh-and-blood beasts of this world. Men armed with hunting rifles have shot at White Things at point-blank range without effect.

Sheepsquatch

A particular White Thing dubbed "Sheepsquatch" has been reported in West Virginia and southwestern Virginia. The Sheepsquatch is about the size of a bear with woolly white hair, and its front paws are more like hands, similar to those of a raccoon but much bigger. The tail is long and without hair. The head features a doglike snout and single-point horns like those of a young goat. It carries a pungent sulfur smell. The Sheepsquatch is rarely seen; most sightings reported over the years in West Virginia have centered in Boone, Kanawha, Putnam, and Mason Counties. A rash of sightings was reported in Boone County in the mid-1990s.

In 1995, a couple driving through Boone County slammed their car to a halt when they spotted a weird white beast in a ditch alongside the road. At first it looked like a woolly white bear. Then they saw that it had four eyes. The creature leaped out of the ditch and attacked the car. The couple sped off. When they got home and examined the car, they found scratch marks on the side.

In 1999, two campers in Boone County heard snorting and snuffling sounds in the woods as they sat by their campfire. They were not far away from their house. A Sheepsquatch suddenly lunged out of the darkness and charged at them. The campers fled toward their house, pursued by the horrible thing. When they cleared the woods, the hairy beast stopped and let out a blood-chilling scream. Then it receded back into the forest. The next day, the campers returned to their site. The trail and the site were torn up as though someone had taken a tiller to the earth.

In Mason County, three people reported seeing what may have been a Sheepsquatch one winter night. They were driving from Huntington to Charleston via Point Pleasant. Heavy snow began falling, slowing their speed. Near Arbuckle, in a lonely and heavily wooded area, they rounded a bend going about five to ten miles an hour on the slick road. The driver glanced to his left and saw a white, furry creature that looked half man and half animal. It had a sheeplike face, ramlike horns, and doglike paws, and it stood upright on its hind, humanlike legs. Stunned, the driver stopped and backed up, not believing what he was seeing. His two friends saw the creature and started screaming. The creature looked straight at the driver and then ran away on its hind legs. One of the passengers was so spooked that he lay down in the backseat the rest of the way home.

A Sheepsquatch may have also been the creature observed in Mason County in 1994 by a young former Navy seaman. The young man had grown up in Gallipolis, Ohio, just across the river from Point Pleasant, West Virginia, the epicenter of the Mothman sightings. He became interested in Mothman and looked for evidence to disprove the entity, figuring in a reverse way that if he could find no disproof, then that would be proof that Mothman was real.

On the night of his encounter, he was out alone chasing down UFO leads along a creekbank north of Bethel Church Road. He saw no UFOs, but instead saw something even more strange. As he walked along the creek, he was startled by the sounds of something large crashing through the brush ahead of him. Since Mason County had little in the way of predators, he thought the creature must be a very big dog or perhaps even a stray cow. Nonetheless, he froze in uncertainty, hoping that he would not be wrong about what was coming through the brush.

The creature that came into view was unlike anything he had ever before seen. It was large and had matted brown-white fur. He could not tell if the fur was dirty white or was brown with a white undercoat. The beast walked on all fours and went to the creek, where it knelt to take a drink, putting out paws that looked more like hands. The head was long and pointed, and doglike in shape, and sprouted large, single-point horns. The creature reeked of sulfur.

Horrified, the young man drew back into the brush, afraid to move or make a sound. After slaking its thirst, the creature crossed the creek and went off toward Sandhill Road. The young man waited until he was certain it was far away and then ran as fast as he could to where he had parked his car.

In making his report to wvtrueghoststories.com, the witness said he did not assume that the sulfur odor meant that the creature was "fire and brimstone," or demonic. Lingering chemical pollution in the TNT area has a sulfur smell, he said, and so perhaps any creatures that lived in the area would absorb the odor.

Demonic or no, it is not the kind of creature one wishes to encounter out in the woods late at night, especially when alone!

The Floating White Thing

A mysterious white creature was seen in July 1973 in the TNT area of Point Pleasant, the epicenter of the Mothman sightings during the 1966–67 wave. This creature, however, looked nothing like the original Mothman. In 1994, a twenty-eight-year-old man reported the encounter to UFO investigator Bob Teets. The young man said that he was seven years old at the time. He was riding in a car with members of his family. They were all returning from a family reunion and were passing by the TNT area.

The witness described the thing as "mostly white, no wings, with real thick, shaggy hair." No face was seen, but the head was about three feet wide.

The creature appeared suddenly alongside the car and floated through the air, following them for a few moments at about sixty-five miles an hour.

The Snallygaster

Maryland's famous flying reptilian, the Snallygaster, ventured across the border into West Virginia on occasion from 1909 to the present, according to newspaper and eyewitness reports. The Snallygaster was first reported in Frederick County, Maryland, in 1909 and was described as reptilian in form with huge wings, a long sharp beak, steel-like claws, a tail about twenty feet long, and a single eye in the middle of its forehead. It screeched and screamed like a locomotive whistle.

Stories quickly spread, and sightings were reported in many locations. The Snallygaster attacked people, drank their blood, and carried off children. Rumors had it that President Theodore Roosevelt and the Smithsonian Institution were interested in tracking one down. The Smithsonian reportedly offered a bounty of $100,000 for one.

The Snallygaster ventured into New Jersey and Ohio as well as West Virginia. Near Scrabble, West Virginia, it reportedly attacked and nearly caught a woman and was seen roosting in a barn belonging to a man named Alex Crow. It disappeared after a battle with three men. A Snallygaster egg was found near Sharpsburg, and two men supposedly built a large incubator in an attempt to hatch it, but failed to do so.

Alas, the Snallygaster was another creation of hoax journalism, intended to boost the sagging sales of the *Middletown Valley Register* in Maryland. The hoax, created by journalists George C.

Rhoderick and Ralph S. Wolf, may have been based on sightings of the Jersey Devil and other reptilian and dragonlike creatures and stories of predatory flying dragons imported by German immigrants. The newsmen may have had entertainment in mind, but they must have been unprepared for the volume of reported sightings that poured into the newspaper from people who truly believed they saw this frightful creature in the skies.

The Snallygaster's offspring surfaced around 1932. It was huge, the size of a dirigible, and had long octopuslike tentacles. After numerous sightings, the creature supposedly met its end when it drowned in a vat of moonshine.

Fictional or not, the Snallygaster continued to be seen, according to periodic reports in West Virginia newspapers. The *Pendleton Times* in Franklin reported that the beast terrorized the family of Kenny Bland in Hopewell on March 1, 1935, and sent Kenny Bland himself up a tree. It reappeared two months later and emitted a "poisonous vapor." It then disappeared for six years and returned on February 14, 1941, to go on a rampage in town. The locals were warned by the howling of "Old Dog Blue," a critter that had previously tangled with the beast. The warning enabled people to flee to their homes when the snarling creature passed through.

The creature's next appearance in Hopewell took place on July 11, 1941, in a surprise attack that claimed the life of Old Dog Blue.

On June 29, 1945, the *Pendleton Times* reported that the "Snoligaster" was back in Hopewell, howling so wretchedly that all the local dogs hid in terror. One deaf dog was killed by the beast. People took cover in their homes.

In April 1946, a coon hunter in Doddridge County captured a "Snoligaster cub" found in a hole by his dog. It was about half the size of a rat, had the claws of a cat, and was covered in fine fur. It was light blue in color with a light yellow face. It had close-set eyes near the end of its nose and ears set low on the jawline. He turned the creature over to two Salem College professors and a representative from the state's Department of Wildlife and Fisheries. Reportedly they decided to raise it, but the fate of the little monster fell into oblivion.

These renewed reports of the Snallygaster probably continued the original fiction, but they did help to anchor the creature into modern crypto mythology and pop culture. In the 1960s the soft drink giant, PepsiCo, created a drink called "The Snallygaster," made out of Mountain Dew soda and vanilla ice cream. Waves of sightings of the Snallygaster occurred in the 1970s, mostly in Maryland, and in 1976 the *Washington Post* created a publicity stunt of an unsuccessful expedition to find a Snallygaster. In 1982, probably in a humorous move, the Maryland legislature added the Snallygaster to its list of endangered species.

Thus the Snallygaster has taken on a life of its own, blurring once again the boundaries between reality and fantasy in the twilight zone of the supernatural.

Death Creatures

he greatest human fear is of death and what lies beyond the grave. Death is portrayed in many guises, often as a monster or creature, stalking the living when their time has come. One of the most familiar figures is the Grim Reaper, a black hooded figure whose face is not visible, and who carries a great scythe for the harvesting of souls. Other horrible figures are death omens, warning the living of impending death. Some might call these figures ghosts or spirits, but "creature" or "monster" are better terms.

West Virginia has its own brands of death heralds and death bringers: the banshee, imported from Celtic folklore; the Raven Mocker, a "night goer" in Cherokee lore; and the white dog.

Banshees

Banshees—hideous, wailing death messengers—came to West Virginia and other parts of America, especially the Appalachians, with Scottish and Irish immigrants steeped in Celtic lore. The Celtic banshee is a kind of fairy; in fact the word "banshee" is Gaelic for "fairy woman." The banshee is attached to families and also places, and it only makes its appearances to herald a death.

In Celtic lore, banshees have different explanations. In addition to being part of the fairy folk, they are said to be monsters sprung from women who died in childbirth, died unbaptized, or were witches in life.

Susan Sheppard, an author in Parkersburg who has researched the Appalachian brand of banshees, told me, "The ancient banshee is a death attendant fairy. Most people think the banshee is a ghost, but it is not—it is a creature."

Banshees are known for their terrible crying, moaning, and shrieking. They are heard more than they are seen, but their keening is unmistakable to those who hear it. When seen, banshees appear in female form. Some are beautiful and some are ugly and hideous. They have long, flowing yellow hair and wear long dresses, cloaks, or burial shrouds that are all white, all red, all gray, or all black. When they are ugly, their hair is stringy and messy, and their clothing is tattered. Their eyes are red from crying over the soon-to-be-dead. The Scottish banshee is usually an ugly crone riding a horse.

Banshees take pleasure in announcing family deaths by singing, crying, or shrieking, the effects of which are bone-chilling. Once a banshee is seen, a fate is sealed. A person must be careful never to insult or harm a banshee, for they can kill others besides the one who is doomed.

Banshees also lurk about certain places in nature, such as streams, or ride about the countryside on spectral horses. Some fly through the air at night, silhouetted against the moon, crying mournfully.

The most famous banshee of West Virginia was attached to the family of Thomas Marr, a Scotsman who immigrated to America in the early nineteenth century in search of a more prosperous life. The Marr family in Scotland lived in the vicinity of the famous Glamis Castle, the oldest inhabited castle in Scotland, dating to the fourteenth century. Glamis has long been reputed to be haunted, not only by ghosts but by a vampiric entity and a "monster" who was a badly deformed human.

Thomas Marr arrived in West Virginia in 1836 and founded a town that was named after him, Marrtown, about one mile south of Parkersburg in Wood County. He married a local woman named Mary, and they enjoyed a prosperous farm. Thomas and Mary were quite happy together, but their prosperity was ruined by the

Civil War (1861–65). They were not alone, for there was scarcely a family across the land that was not affected by the war. The Marrs lost a great deal of property.

Struggling financially, Marr decided to take a job as a night watchman on a toll bridge near Marrtown that crossed the Little Kanawha River. It was miserable duty. Every night, he rode out on his horse to the bridge and stood watch, regardless of the weather. On top of it, the job was lonely and spooky, for the woods around him seemed full of mysterious life.

Marr began to have a spine-chilling experience. Every morning as he rode home, he would see a strange figure riding a white horse. The figure was huddled beneath a hooded shroud, and Marr could not tell if it was a man or a woman. Whenever he rode closer to look, both horse and rider abruptly vanished.

Marr told Mary about the rider. Neither one of them realized the awful truth—that the figure was not a living person, but a banshee, and it had come to warn of the impending death of Marr.

February 5, 1876, was the last day Marr was seen alive. He went to work at the bridge and never came back. Mary awoke with a feeling of great dread. As the hours passed, Mary grew worried. When at last she heard the approach of a horse outside the farmhouse, she was certain it was her husband, late but safe. She ran out to greet him. Instead of Thomas on his horse, she saw a horrible, shrouded figure whose face remained hidden, sitting on a horse that looked to be not of this world. The figure revealed itself as an old woman. She shrieked, "Mary Marr, Thomas Marr has just died. Say your prayers, Lady. I bid you well." Then both figure and horse vanished.

Mary was in shock and disbelief, but the grim message bore out. Within an hour, a man who worked with Marr came to Mary and sadly told her that her husband was dead. Somehow he had fallen into the river. Did he drown, or was he killed by a nighttime robber? Or was he, as some whispered, shocked to death by the banshee?

Mary died many years later at age ninety. The banshee appeared again, but only as a woman's voice that shrieked and cried as Mary's corpse was laid out in her house. Sounds of rattling chains came from the attic.

On down the generations, the banshee was seen by other members of the Marr family. Sometimes its eyes were red. It was always a wretched creature. Eventually the experiences stopped. Perhaps the newer generations lost their connection to the old lore. But do banshees ever really go away—or do we just lose our ability to see them?

Susan Sheppard related a recent banshee experience of a Parkersburg woman, who requested anonymity since it involved family members.

Several years ago "Lisa" awakened one day to the sound of three women crying and wailing. The noise seemed to be coming from inside the house. At first she thought her daughter had stayed home from school and left the television set on. It was a creepy sound, like a cross between sobbing and wailing. She got up and as soon as she reached the end of the hallway outside her bedroom, the crying stopped. Lisa shrugged it off and went back to bed.

She was again awakened by the same sounds. She got up and once again, as soon as she reached the end of her hallway, the sounds stopped.

The next day, Lisa's mother called her with the sad news that her cousin, age fifty, had died of a brain aneurysm. Her cousin had suffered from severe headaches and was taken to a medical facility in Morgantown for testing. She arose from the examination table and fell over, instantly dead of a massive aneurysm.

Lisa and her family attended the funeral. It was more than creepy when she—and no one else—heard the same keening in the background as the service took place.

The Night Goers

Modern-day Wiccans might try to rehabilitate the image of the witch as a do-gooder, but in most societies around the world, witches are evil shape-shifters intent on malevolence. They take on animal, demonic, or monstrous forms in order to work their dark spells. According to Cherokee lore, witches who want to speed the dying on their way are called "night goers," for they move about in animal forms under the cloak of darkness.

The night goers close in on the sick and dying. The most feared is the Raven Mocker, who steals the last breath out of the dying and consumes the victim in order to prolong its own life. The Raven Mocker is so-named because it makes the sound of a raven's call when someone is dying. Powerful medicine is required to keep the Raven Mocker and other night goers at bay, so that the dying can pass in peace. Spirit allies are called upon for protection, and sharpened, blessed sticks are placed point-up around the house. If a night goer attempts an attack, one of the sticks will shoot straight up in the air and come down on the witch's head, striking a fatal blow. The witch will die within seven days.

The White Dog

In Cherokee lore, the sudden appearance of a white wolf heralds a tragic, premature death. Over time, the white wolf became a white dog in Appalachian lore.

The dog is large and powerful in build, a handsome creature despite hair that is somewhat matted and unkempt. The dog shows up in roads, follows people home, and sits at a distance from dwellings, as though waiting for someone. It does not respond to calls or attempts to coax it closer.

The white dog does indeed wait—not for a friend or a lost owner, but for a death. It is always seen by the person who is about to die, and sometimes by others who are close to that person. The dog is invisible to others.

Once the white dog appears, the person marked for death dies tragically within a few days or two weeks. The victim is usually in the prime of life, not old or ill, and meets his or her end in a violent accident. Sometimes the white dog attaches itself to families, much like the banshee. It heralds the deaths of not only family members, but friends or even visitors as well.

Screamers, Flying Manta Rays, and Other Oddities

E very collection of mystery creatures has a few strays and oddities that stand out on their own.

The Roane County Screamer

An unseen beast that makes blood-curdling, demonic growls and screams has been reported in Roane County in the mountains near Spencer. Two hunters said that one winter night the beast came down a hillside and invaded their camp. The frightened men argued about which one of them would make a break for their truck to get a gun. The beast, perhaps just curious, moved back out into the wilderness without aggression. At daybreak the hunters followed the tracks, judging that the creature was large and bipedal. They lost the trail—the creature just seemed to have vanished. At least one other person has reported sighting a large bipedal beast in the vicinity of where the hunters camped.

The Goldtown Screamer

For months in 2010, the mountains near Goldtown in Kanawha County resounded periodically with the eerie screams of an unknown creature. Residents, who were well familiar with the local wildlife, said the screeches did not match an owl, loon, coyote, wolf, turkey, or fox. A representative of the Division of Natural Resources opined that the source might be an owl or loon, but someone at the local sheriff's office volunteered that perhaps the screecher was a ghost.

Mystery shrieks and screams are often attributed to Bigfoot. Some speculated that the Goldtown Screamer was the "second coming of Mothman." Whatever the source, the mystery remained unsolved.

The Blob

No, it wasn't a science-fiction movie, but an all-too real encounter. In 1989, a woman named Pat Q. and her daughter were visiting a friend in Henderson in Mason County. They departed in the afternoon to return home. They drove along the back country roads, enjoying the partly sunny day. As they went down a slope, something "strange" passed in front of their car, going across the road from left to right, about fifty feet ahead of them. It disappeared as it reached the opposite side. Both mother and daughter saw it. Here's what Pat reported:

> What we observed was approximately horse- or cow-sized and it had a white, translucent appearance, without identifiable head, tail, or appendages. It was just a big oval-shaped airy "blob" that you could see through! This thing was like watching a tiny cloud or a mass of fog move on its own. It was flying or gliding quickly across the road and just disappeared on the other side of the road. It moved straight and did not weave or bobble. We only saw it for

maybe five seconds. I had never seen anything like it before and haven't seen another one since.

What was it? Paranormal literature is full of reports of luminosities and nonluminous, fluid shapes of varying sizes that float and fly through the air. Some witnesses have the impression the shapes are intelligent and capable of observing and interacting with them. Others see them as flying, unknown masses that seem to have no awareness of people, as though they are beings going about their business.

I have interviewed witnesses and cataloged many experiences of blobs, orbs, lights, and masses. Some of them are associated with people who seem to be magnets for all kinds of paranormal phenomena and others are stray experiences.

In addition, I have witnessed flying blobs and lights myself in the course of paranormal investigations. In one case I investigated, on a farm property in Pennsylvania just across the border from West Virginia, one of the frequently seen manifestations was a large oval blob, gray-white and semitransparent, that raced across the ground, changing shape as it went, flattening into more of a cigar shape as it gained speed. It would appear suddenly and then vanish as though it dropped into the earth. It seemed to be intelligent, and we (myself, the other investigators, and the principals in the case) surmised that it shape-shifted into other forms that we saw on the property.

Are there odd life forms on our planet that stay mostly beyond the ken of our senses? Perhaps the space around us is full of flying and gliding things we seldom see—unless we are in the right place at the right time.

Flying Manta Rays

Another flying mystery—an airborne "manta ray"—was witnessed on December 3, 2004, near Ashton, also in Mason County. The sighting occurred between 6 P.M. and 7 P.M. on a clear night, after two people, a man and a woman, departed Point Pleasant en route to Huntington. The man was driving. Here is the woman's report:

A friend and I were traveling on Rt. 2 towards Huntington, WV. I was on my way to set up my booth for an art show and my mind was occupied with the booth setup and show logistics. We had just gone over the railroad tracks outside of Ashton WV and were on a long straight stretch of road. There was distant oncoming traffic and the headlights were on. There were no cars behind us in sight. I was in the passenger seat and my friend was driving. I noticed a sudden movement in the sky over the Ohio River to my right in front of the car. It was a greyish, smooth, winged shape. The shape swooped in a figure 8 in front of the windshield and then was suddenly gone to the left of us. It didn't fly out of sight, it was just gone. This happened very quickly, but as I am a visual artist, it was impressed into my memory banks!

Size: Bigger than the car. The wingspread was wider than the 2 lane road we were on. The wings seemed to stretch wider somehow as it did the figure 8 swoop. It was never more than 25 feet away from us as it flew towards the windshield. We thought it was going to crash into the windshield! At one point during the swoop it was only about 5 feet off of the pavement.

Color: Grey, translucent like a jellyfish. As it banked and swooped I could see many angles of it and somehow it looked more transparent as it turned some parts to us. I immediately thought it was like a manta ray. The body was flattish like a manta ray or a bat. The wings were long and smooth and sort of pointed at the tip. I saw no texture or roughness on it, only smooth surface.

Characteristics: Only body and wings—no head, eyes, tail, or feet. It did not look humanoid in any way. On the other hand, it wasn't a bird either. It moved more like something in the ocean would move—Did not flap the wings like a bird, or flutter them like a bat, but stretched them instead. My friend (who alas passed away a year ago) said to him the wings looked ragged like there were pieces coming off of them.

He also said he got a good look at the underneath and it looked grey and smooth. This absolutely was not a machine! It was articulated like a living creature and seemed like something organic.

As I look back on this sighting, I wonder if it was something playing with us—It happened so quickly that the only scary part was when we thought it was going to crash into the windshield. It was so beautiful and strange! It reminded me of a sea creature more than anything else, maybe our air is like water to them.

Another flying manta ray called the "Horton Horror" was reported in Horton in Randolph County. A woman and her daughter saw a manta-shaped "something" that glided along over or near their car.

Researcher Kurt McCoy received an account about a manta ray creature that was so weird he was inclined to discount it as a "campfire story." Perhaps it cannot be dismissed in light of the other accounts above.

According to McCoy, a man driving along a foggy road at night—the location is not given—came upon "a huge ray-shaped thing" that was straddling the road ahead of him. At first he saw only two reddish-orange spots that he thought were bicycle reflectors in the fog. He honked his horn and was shocked to see the "reflectors" blink at him. Then a ray-shaped dark form lifted up off the road and glided over a hill, vanishing into the fog-filled valley below.

Disturbances in the Air

In the 1987 film *Predator*, the bloodthirsty entity is invisible save for a mass of ripples in the air, similar to a shimmering heat wave.

The ripply, moving form is not just fiction: unknown entities appear to us in the same way in some cases. In my own investigations, I have had numerous experiences of air shimmer associated with the manifestation of intelligent presences. These shimmers, or ripples, are not like vague waves of heat rising from hot surfaces, but have shapes that stand out from the space around them. In some cases, I have the impression they are cloaking themselves, and in others I surmise that this is the way certain entities can be perceived by us because of interdimensional limitations we do not presently understand. The fast-moving blob at the farm that I described above also manifested as waves of shimmering energy that distinctly stood out in the airspace. It moved about deliberately as a discrete mass.

I have collected other reports from witnesses of ripply masses, usually in conjunction with investigations of haunted places. I do not think these are ghosts, or remnant energies, but are intelligent entities.

The woman who saw the manta ray along Route 2 had a shimmer experience in 2000. She was driving alone on a one-lane road along the Elk River in Clay County one summer day in the late morning:

For about a mile as I drove, I kept noticing a shimmer in front of the car about 15 feet ahead of the car. This was late morning in the summer. It preceded the car at the same distance for several minutes, then I noticed a shadow on the road too, large and shaped sort of like a bird. I looked up out of the windshield and there was a large crow flying above me. But what I first saw in front of the car was not a shadow, it was a disturbance in the air in front of my car that looked like a heat mirage sort of but was very close. This was a curvy country road right by the river. I had never seen heat mirages on that road before or since. At the time I thought that it was just sort of weird, then very close to that time I had a very lucid dream that I was in my car flying over the river right near the place where I saw the shadow.

Phenomena such as disturbances in the air are likely to be dismissed by most people, and certainly skeptics, as natural environmental conditions—if they are noticed at all. But, as I pointed out above, the very air around us might be swimming with all sorts of mysterious beings who come in and out of focus, depending on the right mix of people, place, and circumstances.

The Hairy Fanged Thing

Bob Teets, a former journalist who has documented many UFO sightings and encounters in West Virginia, found that some UFO witnesses also had encounters with odd creatures—like the hairy fanged thing. One witness was a twenty-nine-year-old woman from Morgantown in Monongalia County, who described an experience she had as a child at age four. She had to spend a great deal of time with her aunt and uncle because of her mother's frequent bouts of illness.

One night, "Angela" (the pseudonym given by Teets) was playing with other children in the kitchen. There was one light on, and the kids were underneath the kitchen table. The adults were outside on the porch. Angela glanced up and saw a hairy monster standing in the doorway. It was about five feet tall, completely covered in long hair, and had fangs and a big nose. She ran screaming out of the kitchen, hollering, "I saw a monster!"

Angela said that according to her mother, that experience altered her personality from a friendly, outgoing child to a withdrawn little girl who was afraid. As she got older, into her twenties, and had roommates, Angela found that her roommates would awaken at night and see shadowy, humanlike visitors in their bedroom. Others saw figures walking around Angela's home.

There followed sightings of mysterious lights in the sky and encounters with alienlike beings. Was the hairy monster associated with the UFO activity, an early visitor perhaps sent by aliens?

Ohio River Serpents and Monster Fish

Sea and lake monsters abound all over the world, and even the Ohio River once had its own giant serpent, according to news reports in 1893. On the moonlit night of June 30, a group of prominent residents of Parkersburg, West Virginia, went out for a boat ride in the river. They reached Neal Island, a sandbar island just offshore of Parkersburg and part of Wood County, where they saw something peculiar in the water. They drew closer, and spied what appeared to be a large serpent, about nine to fifteen feet in length, with eyes like those of a dog, undulating through the glistening water. The boat passengers shouted and screamed, and paddled back to shore as fast as they could.

The serpent was seen again the following night by another group of young couples out for a river joyride. This time, the serpent swam straight for their boat. They reacted much as the first witnesses.

The episodes were reported in newspapers in Parkersburg, Marietta, Ohio, and Gallipolis, Ohio, with comments that perhaps the witnesses had had a little too much to drink and also warnings against swimming in the river.

It is difficult to ascertain what the witnesses really saw, especially considering the dark conditions. Debris floating in black, shiny water might give the appearance of a monster. Whether or not the story was a hoax journalism piece as part of a newspaper war is also difficult to assess. Hoax journalism was prevalent in the late nineteenth century.

Even assuming the original reports were genuine, the story seems to have descended then into what appears to have been hoax journalism. On July 7, a rival Parkersburg newspaper, which had not published the first sightings, carried an article debunking the serpent. Two young monster-hunting men armed with guns rowed out to Neal Island, the article said, and found the culprit. They shot at it several times. When they were able to get close, they discovered that the "serpent" was nothing more than a tree limb with two tin cans tied on one end, which had been mistaken for "eyes." The article scoffed at its rival newspaper and urged "temperance drinks" in the future.

There were no further news reports of the serpent. If the monster was real, perhaps additional witnesses were in fear of ridicule.

Regardless of the reliability of this report, there have been many reports of monster fish in the Ohio River. Some are so huge that they are obvious fish stories—catfish the size of vans and even whales. Monster fish were reported in the wake of the Silver Bridge collapse at Point Pleasant in 1967.

The Enchanted Holler

est Virginia has plenty of hot spots where strange phenomena are not the odd event, but are part of daily living. In many of the areas described in this book, far more happens than the one or two incidents described. People who live in active areas often become so accustomed to the unusual that phenomena are not news but items of passing interest or curiosity: "Oh there goes *that* again," or "Yep, I just saw one of those things again the other night."

I am by no means minimizing the truly frightful, for many of the accounts in this book came from witnesses who were genuinely startled, shocked, and scared. There is much more, however, that goes on in the background in many areas, and the residents know that they are sharing daily space with things not of this world.

When I have the opportunity to spend time in a paranormally active place and get to know some of the residents, I learn quite a bit about the ongoing supernatural history. I am not surprised to find that activity stretches back for generations.

Joey and Tonya Madia live near Fairmont atop a hill that they have christened "New Walton's Mountain." They have a spectacular view from their hilltop and the wooded areas around them. They are by no means isolated, for other homes dot the holler, but no one is close enough to be a "next-door neighbor," so to speak. It's a rough ride off the main road to get to their house, and in the winter, snow sometimes forces them to leave their vehicles outside the holler.

From the time they moved in with their daughter and son, they have found themselves part of a constant play of paranormal activity. Some of it just seems to happen around them, and some of it seems directed at them. "There are things that just move through on their way to somewhere else," said Tonya. "Sometimes things stick around."

The Madias have had a long-standing interest in spiritual and paranormal matters, especially Native American spirituality, and they have investigated around Point Pleasant for Mothman activity. Tonya and Joey have had a life history of paranormal experiences.

The Madias moved into the new house in 2007. Tonya, daughter Jolie, and son Jeremy were the first to occupy it, before the furniture arrived. Tonya noticed a "creepy" feel, especially in the master bedroom. She felt distinctly uncomfortable sleeping alone there and asked Jeremy to come and sleep on the floor until Joey was able to move in.

The discomfort continued, however, even after furniture arrived. One night Tonya awakened to see a ghostly little girl standing by her side of the bed. The little girl visits from time to time, and if Joey must be away on business, Tonya will often sleep on the couch in the living room.

Poltergeist activity happens in the house on an ongoing basis. Small objects disappear without explanation and reappear in strange places. Doors shut by themselves. Jolie hears banging noises in her bedroom often at night, and Jeremy—a skeptic about the paranormal—once saw his bedroom door move noticeably on its own, giving him a bit of a fright.

The family has experienced computer and internet problems and mysterious phone calls in which the caller ID reads out nothing but zeroes, and no one is on the other end.

Small white lights suddenly manifest in the house. "They are like little white laser lights," said Tonya. "They open up and grow in size, and then suddenly blink out."

Once they were settled, the Madias constructed a sweat lodge and conducted a pipe ceremony, inviting the spirits of the land to make themselves known. The entities were happy to oblige. Tonya had met a Native American spirit guide in a meditation, and one night after the pipe ceremony she fell asleep and awakened to hearing the spirit guide calling to her from outside in the back of the house, where the heavier woods are located. Being afraid of the dark, Tonya resisted going outside, then thought better of it since they had extended an invitation to the spirits. Still, she did not go outside, but sat in the living room for a few minutes. For the next three weeks, the house reverberated at night with bangs and thumps against the back side. When a bird committed suicide by flying into a window, and Tonya hit a deer on the road (it limped off), she concluded that the spirits were demanding their attention. The banging noises on the back of the house still happen on an intermittent basis.

Tonya has experienced lucid dreams in which she awakens to find shape-shifting entities trying to get into the house. They always come out of the same place in the woods, in an opening between two large trees, as though there is a portal or gateway. The entity usually starts as a Native American boy and shape-shifts to a Bigfoot-like creature, a half-man, half-mole creature, or an alien. Tonya is always able to prevent them from entering the house.

Mystery lights and shapes are seen in the sky. One night, Tonya lay in bed admiring the full moon, whose light was so brilliant that it lit up the entire sky. While she was gazing out the window across the holler, she noticed a red blinking light moving just over the treetops. It looked like a radio tower light, except that it was moving. She thought it might be an airplane. Then the light suddenly made crazy movements, up and down vertically and then sideways. She got up to get the car keys to drive out and try for a better look, but as soon as she had fetched the keys and looked out the window again, the light was gone.

On another occasion, Tonya was driving down the holler toward home. From the woods in the back of the house, a weird shape rose up into the air. It looked like a huge transparent gray sheet, and it slowly floated and undulated through the trees, which were bare-limbed. It looked big enough to cover about two dozen trees. "Wow, that's new," thought Tonya as she stopped to watch it. After a few seconds, the sheet vanished, never to be seen again.

Mystery creatures and entities appear on the land. Fairies, small folk covered in twigs and leaves, come out at dusk and dawn, and always in the same area. Joey once glimpsed a gray gargoyle-like creature while he was driving out of the holler. Stray cats are rare, but one day Tonya arrived at home to find a massive gray cat with weird-looking, pea-green eyes sitting in the driveway. The cat refused to budge, and something about it made Tonya stay in the car until it departed. Since that time, the gray cat has returned, sometimes with a white cat and a black cat. All four members of the Madia family have seen the cats appear one second and vanish without a trace the next.

Activity goes in cycles. The house and property will fairly buzz with paranormal activity for a few weeks, and then become dormant for a time, as though a battery has to be recharged from some other dimension.

Several years on, the Madias have become accustomed to strange events and sights and take most of them in stride. "You get used to things," said Tonya. Although the master bedroom still has an uncomfortable vibe, nothing feels overtly threatening in the house or on the land, she said.

The Madias' experiences correspond to many cases I have collected over the years. People move to a certain location, and paranormal phenomena start up and never really go away. I have concluded that much of it is generated by land energy and interdimensional portals, as well as the right receptivity among the people present. The phenomena and the presences cannot be banished or exorcised—they are sharing a multidimensional landscape with us.

All of the creatures described in this book may not be accidental visitors to our world, but residents who, under certain circumstances, pop in and out of our awareness. Which makes Planet Earth a very strange place indeed.

BIBLIOGRAPHY

Barker, Gray. *The Silver Bridge.* 2nd ed. Seattle: Metadisc Publishing, 2008.

Berry, Rick. *Bigfoot on the East Coast.* Privately published, 1993.

Bindernagel, John A. *The Discovery of the Sasquatch: Reconciling Culture, History, and Science in the Discovery Process.* Courtenay, BC: Beachcomber Books, 2010.

Brandon, Jim. *Weird America: A Guide to Places of Mystery in the United States.* New York: E. P. Dutton, 1978.

Burchill, James V., Linda J. Crider, and Peggy Kendrick. *The Cold, Cold Hand: More Stories of Ghosts and Haunts from the Appalachian Foothills.* Nashville: Rutledge Press, 1997.

Coleman, Loren. *Bigfoot! The True Story of Apes in America.* New York: Paraview Press, 2003.

———. *Mothman and Other Curious Encounters.* New York: Paraview Press, 2002.

———. *Mysterious America.* Rev. ed. New York: Paraview Press, 2001.

Colvin, Andrew B. *Mothman Speaks.* Seattle: Metadisc Books, 2010.

———. *Mothman's Photographer II.* Seattle: Metadisc Books, 2007.

Feschino, Frank C., Jr. *The Braxton County Monster: The Cover-Up of the Flatwoods Monster Revealed.* Charleston, WV: Quarrier Press, 2004.

Hall, Mark A. *Thunderbirds: America's Living Legends of Giant Birds.* New York: Paraview Press, 2004.

Jones, James Gay. *Haunted Valley and More Folk Tales of Appalachia.* Parsons, WV: McClain Printing, 1979.

Keel, John A. *The Complete Guide to Mysterious Beings.* New York: Tor Books, 2002.

———. *Disneyland of the Gods: An Investigation into Psychic Phenomena and the Outer Limits of Human Perception.* New York: Amok Books, 1988.

———. *Strange Creatures from Time and Space.* London: Sphere Books, 1976.

———. *The Mothman Prophecies.* New York: E. P. Dutton, 1975.

Lapseritis, Jack "Kewaunee." *The Psychic Sasquatch and their UFO Connection*. Mill Spring, NC: Wild Flower Press, n.d.

McCoy, Kurt. *White Things: West Virginia's Weird White Monsters*. Morgantown, WV: Ogua Books, 2008.

Mooney, James. *History, Myths, and Sacred Formulas of the Cherokees*. Fairview, NC: Historical Images, 1992.

Musick, Ruth Ann. *The Telltale Lilac Bush and Other West Virginia Ghost Tales*. Lexington: University Press of Kentucky, 1965.

Sergent, Donnie, Jr., and Jeff Wamsley. *Mothman: The Facts Behind the Legend*. Proctorville, OH: Mark S. Phillips Publishing, 2002.

Sheppard, Susan. *Cry of the Banshee: History and Hauntings of West Virginia and the Ohio Valley*. Charleston, WV: Quarrier Press, 2008.

Teets, Bob. *West Virginia UFOs: Close Encounters in the Mountain State*. Terra Alta, WV: Headline Books, 1995.

Thacker, Larry. *Mountain Mysteries: The Mystic Traditions of Appalachia*. Johnson City, TN: Overmountain Press, 2007.

Wamsley, Jeff. *Mothman: Behind the Red Eyes, The Complete Investigative Library*. Point Pleasant, WV: Mothman Press, 2005.

ACKNOWLEDGMENTS

My thanks especially to Susan Sheppard, Tonya and Joey Madia, John and Tim Frick, Don Keating, Lon Strickler, Loren Coleman, Jeff Wamsley, Frank C. Feschino Jr., Eric Altman, Andrew B. Colvin, Tom Ury, and Lynn Robinson for providing information and expertise as part of my research for this book. I would also like to thank David Houchin, the librarian in charge of the Gray Barker Collection at the Clarksburg-Harrison Public Library, for his invaluable help.

The bibliography lists sources for many of the accounts in this book. Other major sources were PhantomsandMonsters.com, wvtrueghoststories.com, and BFRO.org, the Bigfoot Research Organization online archive.

ABOUT THE AUTHOR

Rosemary Ellen Guiley is a leading expert on the paranormal and supernatural. She conducts original field investigations of haunted and mysterious sites and entity contact experiences. She has written more than forty-eight books, including nine encyclopedias, and hundreds of articles in print on a wide range of paranormal, spiritual, and mystical topics. She is a consulting editor for *FATE* magazine.

In addition, Rosemary makes numerous media appearances and gives presentations at conferences, colleges, and universities around the country. She presents every year at the annual Mothman Festival in Point Pleasant, held the third weekend in September.

Her websites are www.visionaryliving.com and www.djinnuniverse.com. Her email is reguiley@gmail.com.